GHOST
MOTHERS

GHOST MOTHERS

Healing From the Pain
of a Mother
Who Wasn't Really There

Kathryn Rudlin, LCSW

authorHOUSE®

AuthorHouse™
1663 Liberty Drive
Bloomington, IN 47403
www.authorhouse.com
Phone: 1-800-839-8640

Published by AuthorHouse   10/12/2012

ISBN: 978-1-4772-6794-3 (sc)
ISBN: 978-1-4772-6795-0 (e)

Library of Congress Control Number: 2012916835

ACKNOWLEDGEMENTS

Several exceptional people have made it possible for this book to become a reality, and I want to acknowledge each of them. First and foremost is Ariela Wilcox, a woman who came into my life as a literary agent, but became so much more. She has patiently encouraged, guided, edited and believed in this project from the moment I approached her with my dream to write a book about hope, and healing, for un-mothered women.

I've had the good fortune to meet and learn from healers with extraordinary insight and intuition; each came into my life at just the right moment, and contributed to my personal growth in astonishing ways. Heartfelt thanks to Dr. Karyl McBride for her courage, warmth, and passion in helping daughters of narcissistic mothers heal. Gratitude to Dr. Carolle Jean-Murat, better known as Dr. C, for the laughter, wisdom, story-telling, and support she so graciously shares with me, and the profound shift in healing that was her gift to me. Appreciation to Bette Kitnick, MFT, for the compassion, kindness, encouragement and role-modeling she's provided to me over a period of many years. Each of you has provided mothering to me in ways you aren't even aware of, and for which I'm most grateful.

My husband Don Woolley, and my daughter Kendra Woolley, have supported and encouraged my journey for many years. Their enthusiasm for this book to be birthed has helped me stay inspired and on track; their willingness to deal with dinners and dishes has helped too. The love and laughter that our family shares means so much to me, and has provided the security and happiness I didn't get growing up.

My dear friend Marilyn Capra has listened to me kvetch about my mother more times than I'd like to admit, her honesty and intuition in supporting my healing efforts has made a huge difference in my life, her editing and computer skills have helped shape this book into its final form. Betsy Blunsdon, who is a sister to me, has validated my reality since our days together in college, patiently offering her wise counsel whenever I need her. In spite of our physical distance, each has listened, advised and always believed in me.

I am grateful to Dr. Patricia Patton, and once again to Dr. C, for adding their expertise on this topic. This book wouldn't have been possible without the written contributions from my clients, and the courageous daughters I befriended at Dr. McBride's conference; each willingly shared her story based on a desire to help others. To each person that I've acknowledged, I appreciate you more than I know how to express. I hope you know that you've inspired me, and added significantly to the depth and usefulness of this book.

And finally, I want to acknowledge my mother, without whom this book, and my life, would not have been possible.

DEDICATED TO:

The courageous daughters of ghost mothers,
you are not alone.
Listen to the voice inside of you encouraging
you to become visible.

Foreword

Unresolved childhood issues are one of the major causes of unhappiness and dis-ease. Who we are, and what we do as an adult, is the direct result of what happened to us during childhood, and the type of relationship with our parents, especially our mother, in our formative years. Abandonment and neglect wounds can occur in so many ways, such as having a mother, or caregiver, who isn't supportive, or is emotionally unavailable; who shames you, yells at you, or makes you feel that you aren't worthy.

Women abused by a parent have wounds that often manifest in an inability to feel emotions, anxiety problems, depression, an inability to trust, relationship problems, eating disorders, alcohol or drug abuse. Children should expect that their parents are there to protect them, and not to cause them to suffer. It is the deepest hurts that are the most difficult to face, and let go, and so these issues are repressed. With emotional wounds, during stressful moments in an adult's life, especially when feeling rejection, the hurt child will surface, and again experience a deeply ingrained pain that manifests in a variety of symptoms and behaviors.

Whenever we are in a stressful situation, we feel victimized again and we become that hurt child, with a response just like a child—to include arguments, temper tantrums, belligerence, selfishness, and spitefulness. The appearance of symptoms can be likened to the body's intuitive wisdom, reminding the person that these old wounds have to be resolved. Healing unloving or hurtful relationships, especially when it comes to our mother, is the most crucial step to be taken in our lives. I know firsthand because at the age of four, my mother was too poor to raise me, so I went to live with my paternal aunt who was the worst caregiver one could have. It took me having a panic attack at the age of 49 to realize how this childhood situation has impacted my life, and I had to take the steps needed to correct it.

As a board certified ob-gyn and an intuitive healer, I eventually quit the traditional practice of medicine, and created a healing center where women trying to make sense of their lives at midlife can come to heal. Kathryn was one of these women, she came to me exhausted, and frustrated with constantly returning to a state of physical pain. We bonded through our humor and experiences, including having been raised by non-nurturing women.

As I laid my hands on her in the healing room, I was struck by the intense energy coming from her body. I was able to uncover information through that touch, and educated her about how the trauma of her childhood was keeping her from growing up, and that her body was clearly telling her this. She was already on a journey to heal herself emotionally, physically, spiritually, and took my advice to heart. One of the primary tasks was to heal her relationship with her mother—something that sometimes can be very difficult.

I am very proud of how Kathryn decided to take her painful experiences and turn them into a positive opportunity to help others heal. I relate to her decision because of my own journey. This book combines her challenging personal experiences and all that she has learned from counseling others in a compelling and very personal way, to show how to reduce the amount of time spent suffering from similar issues, how to take steps to heal at all levels, and how to take responsibility for moving forward. You will have no choice, if you are willing, than to create the kind of powerful life you want.

Carolle Jean-Murat, M.D., F.A.C.O.G.
Intuitive healer, author, motivational speaker
Founder: Dr. Carolle's Wellness & Retreat Center of San Diego

TABLE OF CONTENTS

INTRODUCTION

This book is based on my personal experience as the daughter of a ghost mother, my journey to heal from growing up this way, and my professional work as a licensed therapist for over 20 years. The imagery of "ghost mothers" came to me in a dream in which I was chasing a woman who had something I desperately needed. I chased her for a long time, and through some bizarre scenery. I chased her until I was out of breath, but when I finally caught up to her, she disappeared in an explosion of white, silky mist.

After waking up I continued to think about this dream until I realized it encompassed how I've spent much of my life, chasing the image of my mother, and longing for her to provide what I needed. Later that day I went through my journal of remembered dreams and found repeated images of chasing, and disappearing, as well as images of fog and mist. But, until this moment, I'd never put all these images together, had not seen in them the symbolism for the issues I'd dealt with for so many years. And then it came to me that this idea of an amorphous mother captured not only the essence of my pain, but that of all daughters struggling to understand a mother who was unable to effectively nurture or love them.

I had finally found a framework, a way to illustrate not only the pain, but also the strategies needed to heal from a mother who wasn't really there, to share what I've learned in my personal and professional journey; what it takes to finally come to terms with who your mother is, and who she isn't. This book is written for all women struggling with issues that, so far, have been difficult to identify. If you are drowning in a confusing, painful relationship with your mother, whether she's currently a part of your daily life or not, you'll find answers in this book. If you had a difficult childhood and can't move past it, this book provides a blueprint for how to do so. If you experience nagging feelings of discontent, but are unable to put your finger on the reason, this information will help you understand yourself in new ways. Increasingly, women in search of a happier, more fulfilled life find that issues to include: strained relationships, low self-esteem, health issues, addiction, anger, or parenting anxiety, directly relate to being haunted by unidentified, or unresolved, issues with a ghost mother. Some women already know this; some will be surprised to discover that the core cause of their current unhappiness may be rooted in these issues.

You will soon discover that this is a simple, yet powerful approach, once you understand some basic concepts—including the fact that joy, peace, and acceptance are well within your reach. The unique perspective of this book is based on the fact that I have been where you are now, and will share with you everything I have learned. Raised by a self-absorbed mother who saw me primarily as a source of adulation, I was born into a situation that confused and overwhelmed me. There was no positive role modeling, or much needed nurturing; in fact I was expected to emotionally take care of my mother, a role reversal that many women with ghost mothers share. Looking back, I see many factors that contributed to my eventual success in being able to stop chasing my ghost mother, come to terms with this reality, and find my own way in the world. My healing journey took a winding, often frustrating direction that included meeting surprising mother figures, trusting my intuition, taking risks, maintaining a sense of optimism, and a considerable amount of good luck. It was many years ago that I began this journey, which at the time I could conceptualize only as: *Something is really wrong here—is there anything that can possibly make it better?*

As I set off on this adventure, did I have tools, a roadmap, traveling companion, deep insight, or anything else to help guide me? No, I did not. I had only myself, a scared shell of a person at the time. But, I did have a conviction, a deeply held belief that there was something I could do about this situation—knowledge and experiences that would help me understand my pain. Having been trained as a therapist, I sought help from other professionals with a similar perspective, but they were unable to provide answers to the problems that were haunting me. No therapist that I worked with made the connection between the difficulties I was having, and the emotional disconnection with my primary role model. Although I was able to locate a handful of books on how to deal with difficult parents, all of which I read and attempted to apply to my own situation, it was not until 2008 that a book was published that finally addressed the reality of my experience.

To a great extent I had to just keep trying to understand my situation, and trust my intuition on this journey. Eventually I found what I was searching for, and it was in no way what I had pictured when I started out. My life improved in astonishing ways, my ghost mother no longer haunted me and I came to understand, and love myself in ways I never thought possible. My situation kept getting better, I continued to feel happier and much to my surprise, I not only survived growing up with a ghost mother, I learned how to thrive, and came to truly appreciate my life.

GHOST MOTHERS is designed to stop your suffering and provide the direction needed to embark on your personal healing journey. I've included stories shared by my clients, and other women who suffer from the pain of being raised by a ghost, and while the details that describe these illusive mothers may differ from your own, I suspect the overall themes will be eerily similar. The result is the book I wish I'd had during my healing journey, as it contains the help that I needed from someone who knew what I was going through, who could provide insight, reassurance, humor, and practical steps to move forward. Many of the women I now have the pleasure to talk to, and work with, feel confused, discouraged, angry—and rightly so; their response is easy to understand. What is more hidden are the benefits of digging deep to mine the gems of growing up this way, because ultimately this journey is not about your mother, it is about you. There is so much to life beyond growing up with a mother who is more problematic than nurturing. Together we will explore the ways lack of mothering has impacted you, and then I'll share with you what you need to know, and do, so that you are no longer haunted by your past. My goal is to provide the information needed to show you how to transcend the pain of being raised by a mother who wasn't really there, by providing validation, illumination, and specific healing strategies to decrease the amount of time you spend feeling miserable, believing that *you* have done something wrong. The havoc that is wreaked by a ghost mother is invisible to those outside the immediate family, and this book is intended to bring this problem out of the shadows, while providing hope and healing to those who suffer from growing up this way.

There will be a period of much needed healing, absolutely, but there doesn't need to be an extended period of suffering, not once you understand you're haunted by issues your mother wasn't able to resolve—and quite possibly her mother before that. Knowledge, and deep understanding, will finally set you free from the pain of your past, and go a long ways towards ending the legacy of a ghost mother unable to raise her daughter in nurturing ways. The problems you are currently experiencing will make sense once you clarify the core cause; recognize (perhaps for the first time) that you are not making this up, overreacting, or being too sensitive. Ghost mother issues impact us on a deep, primal level, but once understood, these issues have the potential for deep healing, and can propel you into a new reality you may not even be able to imagine at this point. Join me on the journey to heal from this insidious pain.

What's included in this book:

Chapter 1 tells my story of growing up with a ghost mother, the impact this had on me, and the steps in my journey to understand, and heal from this illusive issue.

Chapter 2 explores the qualities of a ghost mother, and differentiates these issues from normal mother-daughter conflict. This chapter includes three quizzes to help define the extent to which your mother is a ghost.

Chapter 3 describes a scary type of ghost mother, one who is self-absorbed and cruel, and explores the impact of growing up with the role-reversal of trying to emotionally care for, and please this type of mother.

Chapter 4 explores why it hurts so much to grow up with a ghost mother, the reasons you continue to be haunted by this childhood wound, and describes the problems that develop when you attempt to avoid dealing with this pain.

Chapter 5 shows how to stop being haunted by a ghost mother, and held back by the problems she's been unable to resolve. The information in this chapter will help you to view your mother in more realistic terms.

Chapter 6 introduces ghost-busting strategies to empower you in healing from a ghost mother by describing the step-by-step process needed to heal, and presenting a variety of techniques and strategies to help you do so.

Chapter 7 takes you beyond surviving a painful past, and discusses how to find the hidden gifts of growing up this way, while describing the strength, compassion and insight that develops during the process of healing.

Let's get started with our exploration of the painful legacy of growing up with a ghost mother, the impact it's had on you, and how to move past this pain. Note that at the end of each chapter I've included an exercise to get you involved in the healing process right away. Do these exercises as you go along so that when you get to the ghost-busting strategies in chapter 6, you'll know what to expect, and will already have a good idea of which approaches work best for you.

CHAPTER 1
MY STORY

**The many years spent chasing
my ghost mother.**

The ghosts you chase you never catch.
~ John Malkovich

Tales of Growing Up With a Ghost

*. . . and then the huge, ugly monster opened his mouth
wide, revealing hideous fangs, and tried to eat the little
girl.*

*I woke up trembling; afraid the monster in my dreams was
still close by, and eager to start gobbling me up. Gathering all my
courage I ran down the hall to where my mother was sleeping,
seeking safety and solace. Still shaking, I described to her the
monster in my dream, and my fears that it was me he longed to
eat. "Can I sleep with you?" I pleaded.*

Grudgingly, my mother made room in the bed for my tiny frame as she issued the following instructions, "You are not to keep me from sleeping—lie there, be still, don't move."

So I did as I was told, I stayed on my back, arms against my sides, trying not to move a muscle; afraid I would be screamed at, and dismissed, if I dared to again interrupt my mother's slumber. I wanted to move around a bit to get more comfortable, but feared doing so. Instead I did my best to be a "good little girl." I remained in the space assigned to me by my mother, who obviously knew more about these things than I did.

I lay stiffly beside her, trying not to move a muscle, with my fists clenched, and my mind filled with images of monsters. I now feared falling asleep, because then I might move, wake up my mother and get sent back to my room where, I was certain, I'd make a delicious meal for a monster. What I really wanted was for my mommy to reach out and comfort me, to hold me in her arms. I wanted her to reassure me there would be no return visits from the ugly monster, that she would make sure I was taken care of. I wanted this but did not get it; what happened instead is that she turned away from me, and quickly fell asleep.

Instead of feeling comforted I was now doing everything possible to make myself invisible as I lay next to my mother, doing my best imitation of a statue, in order to not disrupt her slumber. It was clear I needed to keep my fears and discomfort to myself, so I kept my body rigid, believing that I'd done something wrong, that I was silly to be afraid of monsters, that it was selfish (a word my mother repeatedly used to describe me) to want to be comforted, that I was taking up space that was rightfully hers.

On this night my father was away on a business trip, so I only had my mother to turn to. Through this experience, and similar ones, I learned at a young age what the rules were for growing up in this family. I was not to expect comfort, not be a nuisance, and if I was having a problem, I needed to figure it out on my own. Be self-sufficient, be a good girl, keep your problems to yourself; these were the messages I received from an early age. Seeking comfort from my mother that night, expecting reassurance that I'd done the right thing by coming to her for help seemed like a reasonable assumption on my part and now having raised a child; I know that it was. What I was told, the way she acted when I sought comfort conveyed to me that because I was scared by my nightmares, I was bothersome to her, and this became a theme that would echo throughout my life.

My sense of being loved and cared for didn't improve as I continued to grow up, particularly not with the addition of two younger siblings, and the death of my father from a sudden heart attack when I was 18 years old. This early memory of not being comforted from my monster dream provided the foreshadowing for how I would grow up. Remembering it, feeling the confusion, sadness, and misery that I was forced to hold in as a young child eventually helped me work through the painful issues I faced growing up with a significant lack of nurturing.

Although I eventually studied psychology and social work, and became a licensed therapist in my efforts to figure out why I couldn't get what I needed from my mother, I didn't develop an understanding of what drove her angry, self-absorbed behavior for many years. I just knew that I didn't feel comfortable with her, that she wasn't warm or loving, didn't listen, and rarely focused on what I needed; instead the focus was always on her. Nothing I ever did pleased her, and she was frequently angry with me for something I did, or didn't do. For the next several decades I tried to convince myself that our relationship wasn't really that bad, and accepted all the blame and responsibility for the issues I did acknowledge.

As I look back on my childhood, I see that to those who viewed it from a distance, it might seem almost idyllic, Mom, Dad and three kids living a middle class, suburban lifestyle. My father worked as a physicist in a professional job, my mother stayed home with the kids, what was there to complain about? And yet there was a considerable amount of pain, and confusion, behind the superficial outer wrapping of our lives together. Billy Crystal captured this well in his skits on Saturday Night Live when he said: "It's better to look good than to feel good." The happy family my parents tried to portray really wasn't all that happy, and in spite of how things may have looked to friends and relatives, I grew up needing my mother to be very different than who she was.

When I was 7 years old my youngest brother was born. A nanny was hired to take care of me, and my other brother—and we fell in love with her. I don't remember her name but I do remember the essence of her, the loving manner in which she took care of us. Every night we looked forward to the colorful stories she told, the warmth and caring she extended to us as she sat close, and mesmerized us with her tales. When her time at

4

our house was over, I missed her immensely and still remember her fondly. Rather than being pleased that we were so well taken care of, our mother seemed angry that we liked the nanny so much, and did not want us to talk about her after she left.

It's significant that there have been so many mother figures in my life that have made a dramatic impression on me. It's clear I wasn't getting what I needed from my own mother for this to happen, a fact that became even more apparent when other adult female figures were far more nurturing, and tuned into me, than she ever was. In my childhood it was my Aunt Bessie who helped provide what I needed, she was maternally related and lived in Alabama. Every summer she spent several weeks with us, and although I remember her being quite old, I loved her dearly and looked forward to our time together. I was her favorite; we put puzzles together, walked around the neighborhood, talked, laughed, and I felt very special when I was with her. I wasn't allowed to wake her up in the morning, so I sat on the steps outside her room waiting to hear sounds that indicated she was awake. Then I could go into her room to greet her, that's how eager I was to see her each day. The strength of these memories points to how desperate I was for motherly attention, as well as feeling accepted and loved for who I was. When my dear aunt died, I inherited her wedding ring, and the diamond was set into my ring when I got married; so happily she continues to be with me in spirit.

As summer waned, and a new school year loomed on the horizon, I dreaded the ordeal that ensued while shopping for clothes with my mother. When we went shopping she told me what looked good on me, and what I wanted to buy. While I rarely agreed with her opinions I didn't dare argue with her because I would be screamed at and criticized if I did. I was extremely eager to please my mother so that she would love me, and to avoid having her make a scene. If this meant wearing an ugly wardrobe, I was willing to do so, it was a small price to pay. I had a strong aversion to the color red (much too bold and bright for someone trying to be invisible) but my mother loved it, and always picked out clothes for me in this color, which I dutifully wore in my efforts to make her happy. For years I played the part of the good little girl, but the fact was that I didn't have much to show for it.

As I grew older it continued to be extremely important to me to try to find ways to connect with my mother, and I blamed myself when I didn't succeed. It seemed that I couldn't define, or feel good about myself, until I gained her love and positive attention; so I tried hard to please her, bending over backwards to do what she told me to do, attempting to meet her needs so that she would embrace me as the daughter she loved, literally and figuratively. This became a vicious cycle in which I was never successful, and over time this pattern led me to view myself as a dismal failure. If I constantly disappointed my own mother, then something in me must be sorely lacking. So I kept trying harder, thinking that with continued effort she would eventually respond to me in the ways I needed. When I admitted to myself the negative feelings I had towards her, I felt awful, thinking perhaps I *was* the ungrateful daughter she said I was, and so I tried to ignore these feelings, hoping they would go away, keeping them a dark secret that I didn't share with anyone.

My father was a stabilizing but not very strong influence in our family, kind of a behind the scenes guy, who let my mother run the show. I suspect he kept her happier and more emotionally balanced than I realized at the time, but due to the demands of his work schedule he traveled a great deal, making him a somewhat illusive presence in my life as well. My mother resented this, and complained bitterly because he often wasn't home to help take care of us. He was better at showing affection than she was, usually through silly bear hugs, as a way of making physical contact. When he was home he usually tried to have fun with us, while most of the interactions with my mother were serious, and fraught with tension. When he died suddenly from a heart attack, the difficulties I was having with my mother got considerably worse. Although there were supportive family members and friends in the picture, she assumed a stance in which she viewed herself as being completely alone, and the only one impacted by his death. Many years later she told me, "You can't possibly know what it was like." Well I was there too, deeply affected by this sudden loss, confused, emotionally overwhelmed, and now without any semblance of a functioning mother. I needed comforting and reassurance that our family would be okay, but instead my mother went into victim mode, and the emotional drama she created was substantial. It was a terrible time. The toughest part were her frequent threats to kill herself, threats that expressed her sense of despair, but were also disturbingly effective in getting me to do exactly what she wanted, including staying at home rather than spending time with my friends. I was traumatized by the thought of losing my remaining parent, so I succumbed to her demands, worrying about her constantly, while at the same time resenting her for focusing only on herself, ignoring my pain, and that of my siblings. Many years later I attempted to discuss this with her, and was told it had never happened. Later she wrote to me that "... if it did happen, I wouldn't be the first widow to have a hard time losing her husband," which totally discounted the horror of what it was like to have my father die suddenly, and then my mother threatening to leave me as well; didn't she love me at all?

I stayed close to home for several years, determined to help my mother, and still hoping to create a connection with her. But the reality was that after doing things for her constantly, I was criticized for my efforts. Nothing was ever done to her satisfaction, met her standards, or made her happy; I just didn't measure up. I was now in my early twenties, a time when I needed to separate from my mother, but instead I felt trapped taking care of her, with no acknowledgement for doing so, and no time for myself. Finally, I got fed up and left the East Coast to attend graduate school at the University of Denver. This move helped me gain a healthier perspective on my life, but my mother continued to make demands, and raged at me for not calling often enough. During a time when I needed something from her, having been hospitalized with a serious pelvic infection, she barely paid any attention to what I was going through. But in spite of all I've recounted, it wasn't until the birth of my daughter that it *really hit me* that there were substantial issues between me and my mother that I had to address and deal with.

I married a wonderful man at the age of 29, and together we created a relationship in which I received the unconditional love, attention, safety, and stability that I didn't get growing up. Seven years later Don and I were having a baby, and my mother claimed to be "thrilled." She came to help us after the baby was born, but before even entering the house made her intentions clear by announcing, "I don't do nights," and demanding that we put a fan in her room to help drown out the sound of crying. Of course, with a new baby this is the kind of help exhausted parents need, but instead we now had to be careful not to wake up Grandma. I was angry, and annoyed, that after talking for years about how happy she'd be when I "finally gave her a grandchild," she showed up with no intention of helping with this new baby.

Far more troubling was the fact that she seemed fake, and awkward when interacting with our new daughter. Having always believed that it was my fault we didn't have a good relationship, I was surprised, and heartbroken, that it was so difficult for her to develop a bond with this beautiful baby. From the day she arrived to "help," she wanted to control her role as grandma; including discussions of what the baby should call her. I'd had a C-Section, and experienced other serious complications, but she expressed no concern for how I was feeling, or healing, and offered no motherly advice on feeding the baby, or any of the other new tasks we were attempting to master. It appeared she was in residence to show off her status as grandma, and that was about it. This was behavior I couldn't continue to ignore. It hit me like a ton of bricks as I looked at my mother from the perspective of a new mother; I had fallen head over heels in love with our new daughter. Suddenly I knew, deep in my heart, that my mother had never felt the same way about me.

The Healing Journey That Led Me to Write This Book

When I became a mother I certainly came to appreciate how difficult it is to raise a child, but I also saw that the issues between us went far beyond normal mother-daughter conflict. Now I could see in her interactions with Kendra that she couldn't connect with her either. It was more of a theatrical performance in her role as grandma, and now I suspected that her efforts to mother me were a superficial performance as well, and not a very good one. The relationship between us continued to spiral downward, from my perspective. It seemed that she bitterly resented the demands my husband and child placed on my time and attention, rather than embracing these loving additions to my life.

In my late thirties I needed to have a laparoscopy (a surgical diagnostic procedure) to determine the reasons for ongoing abdominal pain. I realized how little I could count on my mother when I decided it made no sense to tell her I was scheduled to have this procedure. I knew from past experience that she wouldn't be supportive, that in fact I would be required to call with updates, so that she "wouldn't have to worry." Once again it would become all about her, so why bother? After years of being the dutiful daughter who always put her needs first, I was having an increasingly difficult time with her constant complaints, demands and controlling behavior. Now I realized how one-sided our relationship was, and increasingly dreaded having any contact with her. Her visits were filled with tension, and visiting her was even worse. There was so much stress that I was having physical ailments, to include colds and stomachaches, before and after spending time with her—somehow my body knew better than to hurt while I was with her, when I was expected to constantly meet her needs and ignore my own. Increasingly, I avoided her calls and made up stories about not being at home, rather than having to deal with her.

At a time when I was experiencing so much distress, I heard about a seminar with a title that intrigued me, **Finishing the Business With Mother**, and decided to attend. The facilitator was a well-known family therapist named John Bradshaw who frequently shared his wisdom on PBS specials. I knew I needed to attend, but at the same time I was terrified to face these issues, and feared what I might learn in taking this step. I signed-up anyway, and it was the first time I allowed myself to do two things: talk openly with strangers about the issues I was having with my mother, and seriously consider the possibility that my hope of having a positive, loving relationship with her was never going to happen.

While listening to others describe similar struggles, I got in touch with the reality that I was being emotionally, and verbally abused by my own mother, a person I expected to have my best interests at heart but who was far more likely to scream at me than to help me. I began to understand my deep sense of powerlessness in being able to make positive changes in our relationship, and finally admitted to myself that I could not go on like this. My well-meaning efforts to get along with her had not garnered positive results after four decades of trying, and this ongoing pattern was negatively impacting my physical and mental health, my family, my work, my sense of self, and my outlook on life. Inspired by this seminar I decided to take a 3-month break from my mother, news that was difficult to deliver to her, but somehow I managed; at this point it didn't feel like I had much choice. I was exhausted from trying to please her, and disgusted with feeling distraught after every interaction.

What a feeling of relief it was for me to have the opportunity to experience what it was like not to have her constant, unpleasant presence in my life. I didn't have to make up stories to avoid talking to her, I didn't get screamed at, I was finally able to focus on myself. I discovered that I didn't miss her, and it occurred to me there was nothing positive to miss, which was quite a revelation. I came to realize that what I did miss was what I'd always longed for, but never seemed to get, a mother who nurtured and truly cared about me. After two months she insisted I talk to her again, and I relented, hoping that perhaps she'd made positive changes during this time, and that at the very least, she now recognized our interactions needed to change if we were to continue to have a relationship.

With this break came a significant shift within me; I now clearly saw the negative impact of this relationship on my life, and vowed to open myself up to understanding what the problems really were. My perceptions had changed, and continued to do so. The contrast between how I felt when I wasn't in contact with her, and how I felt when I agreed to let her back in my life was substantial. For a brief period I had experienced taking care of myself, not being criticized or yelled at, not being pulled into her problems, and it was no coincidence that I'd been sleeping better and feeling happier. Now, I was ready to really deal with this situation; it was time for me to delve into these dynamics with the help of a therapist.

From the moment I met Bette Kitnick, MFT, a therapist in Encinitas, CA, I sensed she would be able to help, and it felt terrific to finally vent the feelings and concerns that I'd held in for so long. She listened to everything I had to say, nothing shocked her, as I feared it might. Finally, I began to trust someone enough to fully express my pain, and over time I felt safe enough to peel away each layer of what I'd been through, and understand the impact it had on me. I vented, I raged, I cried and then slowly, patiently, we began the process of working through it all, grieving the childhood I'd never had, the mother I'd longed for.

Eventually it became clear that pathological narcissism was driving her behavior, (more about this in chapter 3) and that this disorder was the reason my mother couldn't emotionally connect with or relate to me. Even in this long-term therapeutic relationship, I was the one who eventually figured this out, somewhat by accident. While working on my continuing education credits, I came across an interview with Sandy Hotchkiss, LCSW about personality disorders, in which she seemed to be describing my mother. I consulted with her via phone, describing my mother's behavior and the problems between us. She clarified what might be going on, and suggested resources, including her book, **Why Is It Always About You?** *which helped me understand the core cause of my mother's difficult behavior. I took this information to Bette, and because she possessed the qualities I'd always wanted in a mother to include kindness and compassion, we were able to work further with this significant insight, finally putting together the pieces of this puzzle.*

With her help I began to see how my deep desire to have a loving mother had blinded me to the reality of who my mother really was. Then we explored how I could begin to heal, and feel better, by identifying the many ways I was beating myself up with "if only" thinking. If only I was a better daughter, if only I'd done the things my mother asked me to do, if only I could figure out the right thing to say to her that would get a positive response, if only . . .

I was beginning to see that in my quest to please my mother I had completely lost sight of myself. There was a great deal of work to be done, but I was now able to view this situation more realistically, to examine my role in it, and see what I could, and couldn't be held responsible for; with Bette's help, I was starting to get myself on track, or so I thought.

Physically I was now experiencing some serious problems, and this turned out not to be a coincidence, these issues were directly related to decades of dealing with maternal angst. Years of hormonal imbalance had been created from the stress I'd been under, the anxiety I experienced, the doubts I held about myself, and all of this had taken its toll on my body. In my late forties I suddenly started having migraines, in which auras came on suddenly, followed by intense headaches that lasted several days, and left me exhausted. Lying in bed, in the dark, praying for this pain to diminish, I found myself crying as I longed for a mother who would comfort me, instead of making me feel worse.

When a brain scan showed no obvious problems I began tracking the onset of the migraines, and discovered they usually began several days before getting my period. Eventually I was able to reduce their frequency by taking bio-identical hormones, but I also began to notice a pattern in which the migraines started, or worsened, when I communicated with my mother. I knew that this was a strong sign from my body, and began to further reduce the amount of contact I was having with her. After taking the hormones for two years, and feeling much better, I began to bleed with great frequency, and was experiencing intense cramps. The doctors I was working with felt this response was due to the hormone replacement, and that they "just needed to find the right balance." I was starting to understand how the emotional pain I had experienced, the longing I'd held on to for so long, and the feelings I'd been reluctant to express had wreaked havoc with my body.

At the same time I was trying to correct my painful health problems, I was also dealing with issues that my daughter, now a young teenager, was having in response to a complicated case of mononucleosis. During this time, which ended up lasting several years, I wasn't able to work, and spent hours each day comforting her, and coordinating efforts to diagnose and treat her health problems. What I was dealing with on a daily basis worsened my health issues, as I was very worried about my daughter, and experienced considerable frustration that she wasn't getting better. To make matters worse, this situation triggered deep feelings of inadequacy within me. I began to question my value, and effectiveness as a mother since my daughter was in pain, and I wasn't able to provide what she needed. Eventually, we did find answers to Kendra's health problems, and I began to focus on my own. In spite of trying numerous healing strategies, I ended up having a hysterectomy to remove the numerous fibroids that were growing inside me.

At this point I was much more aware of the fact that my body was responding to the trauma that I'd experienced growing up. It seemed to me that these fibroids represented the pain that hadn't been dealt with, and by the time I had the surgery I was eager to have them removed, feeling that a physical and emotional burden was literally lifted from me. After a period of recovery I was feeling really good, but for reasons no one could understand, I began having insomnia because my calves throbbed when I went to bed, and I couldn't get comfortable enough to fall asleep. Initially I thought I had developed restless leg syndrome, but when this diagnosis was not confirmed, I announced to myself, "I'm going to do something different than what I've done before."

The next day I opened a magazine and saw a beautiful, wise face, the face of a healer unlike anyone I'd experienced before so I did what the article encouraged, I called and began talking to a woman I had difficulty understanding. Dr. Carolle Jean-Murat is from Haiti, an accent I was unfamiliar with. She talks fast, and I was very tired, so I was making out every third word and thinking this was a waste of time. A voice inside me suggested trying harder to focus, and when I did, her words became clearer, and there was a healing energy in her words that began to soothe me. After talking for a while, she invited me to spend several days at her healing retreat. This was way out of my comfort zone, my inclination was to say, "thanks, but no thanks," but I needed to get some sleep, and next thing I knew I had accepted her offer.

I spent three days with Dr. Carolle during which time she offered healing to me in ways I'd never experienced before. She is an amazing woman, a certified ob-gyn with deep bloodlines to Haitian healers—her grandfather was a Voodoo priest. In her work as a traditional medical doctor she was increasingly able to tune into what was causing the health problems her patients presented. We walked in the beautiful gardens, and talked a great deal (she is much easier to understand in person) and soon I knew I'd met a kindred spirit as she described having been primarily raised by her aunt, a woman who meant well, but seemed to have had issues similar to my mother's.

Dr. Carolle had a delightful way of educating me about the ways the emotional trauma I'd gone through were manifesting in my body. Learning from her gave me so much hope; here was a brilliant, highly intuitive woman who had surmounted numerous obstacles. It was during this time that the connection was made between lying rigidly next to my mother as a child, not getting the comfort I needed, and the physical problems I was currently experiencing.

"In many ways you are still that 4-year old, trying to get what you needed from your mommy," she said to me. I really didn't like hearing this; it made me feel worthless and angry, to

hear that I was a woman in her fifties who was having problems because she couldn't get past wanting, and needing, her mother. In my heart though, I knew that she was right.

With this unique healing experience I began to come to terms with how pervasive the issues were that I'd developed in chasing my ghost mother for so long. My time with Dr. Carolle gave me increased hope, and direction. She helped me recognize that I'd been defining myself as someone who'd been victimized, and needed help from others, rather than focusing on the strength, and intuition, inside of me. By her example, Dr. Carolle taught me there was a considerable amount I could do to re-focus from trying to gain my mother's love and approval, to gaining my own.

Healing at a Deeper Level

I made a difficult decision to cut off all contact with my mother after repeated efforts to create change in our communication failed. The health problems that worsened when I tried to connect with her convinced me that I wouldn't heal as long as I continued to engage in this toxic relationship. In my efforts to learn more about narcissism, I came to understand my mother was doing the best she could, that she struggled to get her own needs met. I knew it was going to take a considerable amount of effort, of looking at this situation from a different perspective, for me to successfully move forward on my own.

I was able to make an important shift when I stumbled across the spiritual aspects of healing, and I did so having no idea this is what I was doing. I was introduced to the Unity Center of San Diego when my friend Marilyn suggested we attend an event called Mantra. This sounded rather cosmic, but turned out to simply mean singing along to guitar music (some with unusual lyrics) in a setting with soothing lighting; I felt calm and happy when it was over. This experience was so profound, and yet so simple, that it encouraged me to explore spiritual teachings as a way to heal on a deeper level. I began to attend the services, and learned a great deal from the emphasis on taking responsibility for our choices, and living a conscious life. Inspired by this approach, I now was taking better care of myself, setting aside time to clear my mind, and paying attention to the information that came up during this time. I began to trust this wisdom, and listen to it in my daily life. I broadened my longing for a mother to a longing to better understand the universe, and myself, and I was learning how to do so. I began to think differently about where I'd come from, to see that while my mother had birthed me, I was part of a much larger universe; filled with infinite possibilities. Developing my spirit added to my ability to grow and accept myself, it's filled me with a sense of hope, and attending services at the Unity Center provides me with a readily accessible environment in which to relax, reflect, and heal.

In my work as a therapist I had often relied on my intuition, on the thoughts that came up during a session, and I was starting to see that this inner wisdom continually had provided me with the optimism to navigate this painful situation with my mother. Now I was learning ways to fan this spark so that it produced a flame; I was discovering the power that existed within me. Instead of continuing my failed efforts to connect with her, I was learning how to connect with myself. I began to see the painful interactions with her as life lessons, and this helped me develop a sense of compassion for her; and paved the way to finally developing a sense of peace and acceptance.

I now was able to interpret my grief differently, and understand that while I didn't have much impact on the outer experiences with my mother, I did have choices in terms of my inner experience; to include my thoughts and feelings. The concept of a higher power has provided me with comfort and nurturing, and introduced me to deeper truths I may not have explored if I hadn't gone through this pain. The spiritual concepts I've embraced remind me not to take myself too seriously, and to remember the profound forces that keep all life moving forward.

True to form, the next stop on my healing journey came about in an unexpected way, and at a point when I wasn't looking for any more help. Marilyn had relocated to Denver, and she called to tell me about a conference advertised on TV.

"It's for daughters of narcissistic mothers," she explained.

"I'm getting kind of tired of learning about narcissists," I responded.

"Just check it out," she encouraged. "Check out Dr. Karyl McBride."

Searching through my collection of books on this subject, I realized this psychologist had authored the book that most closely mirrored my own experience, **Will I Ever Be Good Enough?** Now I was intrigued, not only would I get to meet and learn directly from her, she was encouraging therapists to attend, and be trained in her recovery model. I was moving in a direction where I wanted to combine my recovery, personal experience, and skills as a therapist to help un-mothered daughters, but up to this point I'd been reluctant to take this step. *Did I really know enough to help someone else?* I asked myself. *How could I describe the steps that had helped me? Would the emotions that came up in listening to similar stories overwhelm me?*

Denver is a large city, but with the synchronicity I was coming to expect, when I looked into the conference, it was being held near where Marilyn lives, so I could stay with her, and enjoy home cooked meals, discussion, and de-briefing each evening. Having no idea what to expect from what I imagined would be an intense experience, I couldn't have been more surprised at how the conference unfolded. Women from across the U.S., and a few from other countries, accepted Dr. McBride's invitation to come together for a shared experience of healing.

It's difficult to describe the changes that took place within me in this setting, one that further explained my experiences growing up. Dr. McBride, also the daughter of a narcissistic mother, made this a unique opportunity to talk to other women about the issues that had profoundly impacted our lives. It was a liberating experience, to bond with someone you just met, already knowing so much about her pain, but also sharing a sense of hope because each of us had already overcome incredible odds to be there in the first place. The extent of this validation was significant for each of us, having been raised in a family where it's unclear what's really going on, when the situation doesn't feel right, but it's difficult to understand what's causing this.

I had expected maybe 10-20 people at this conference, over 100 attended. Having grown-up in families where there was a strong message, "what happens in this family stays in this family;" it was a life changing experience to share openly, and honestly. Being part of a large group of women determined to come to terms with the pain of growing up with a problematic mother was a revelation for me, after having felt alone with this pain for so long. The commonalities of what we'd experienced were striking; our mothers had treated and interacted with us in much the same ways; based on what they needed, not what we needed. Even more intriguing were the effects of being mothered this way. For most of us the results were eerily similar, and this is what we'd come to work on.

The first conference day was difficult, as I revisited many childhood experiences and was reminded of how much I'd suffered. During the next two days I came to realize how much I had truly healed from my pain, and how passionately I now felt about using my experience to offer hope to others. I saw that there was no reason for lengthy periods of suffering, no reason to take responsibility for problems we didn't create, and significant hope for moving beyond this pain.

If I Knew Then What I Know Now

As I'm writing this I recognize that what I've been through has been a long and winding journey, and partly this is because there were so few resources at the time when I started my journey in 1997. Other women have experienced this frustration as well, slowly this situation is starting to improve and more information is available, but still not enough. What I've learned has taught me short cuts to healing from a ghost mother that I will share with you. I don't recommend you take the circuitous route I've taken; I now know there are easier ways to stop being haunted, stop chasing your mother, and to get on with your life.

So does my ghost story have a happy ending? I think the answer depends on your perspective, on how you choose to view what I've shared. In my view, this story ends better than I could have imagined when I started this journey. I've learned why I couldn't get what I needed from my mother, I've grieved this deep loss, and discovered how to get the nurturing I need from other sources. Not only have I survived my ghost mother's lack of caring and concern, I've learned how to thrive due to the emotional, physical, and spiritual healing that I've embraced.

What I haven't managed to do is find ways to have a healthy connection with my mother, and it is this reality that partly inspired me to write this book. As I look back with the knowledge I now possess, I see so many things I would do differently. But to be honest, I'm not sure that what I've learned could change how things played out between us. Yet, I can't help wonder what *might* have happened if I'd known sooner that she was a ghost, and had recognized how deeply wounded she was. Based on what I've learned, I can now pass on what I wish I had known many years ago.

I know only too well that not being able to have a fulfilling relationship with your mother is an intensely sad situation, and it doesn't help that I'm writing this with Mother's Day on the horizon. Mothers are special people, at least they should be, but if yours is a ghost, this becomes a relationship filled with pain, and problems. My experience has taught me that it doesn't have to be this way, and this is what we will explore together. Developing knowledge about your ghost mother invests you with a considerable amount of power, power that can keep you from being haunted for the rest of your life.

This book encourages you to face the reality of having a ghost mother, and offers direction for embarking on your healing journey. I think what's most important is to not lose sight of yourself because you're so busy chasing her. If I knew then what I know now, I would have let go sooner, and stopped trying to get from her what she didn't have to give. Seeing your ghost mother as she really is has the potential to improve your relationship with her, and guarantees that you'll improve your relationship with yourself. Although I didn't find a positive relationship with my mother, I did develop a deep relationship with myself, with my world, and with others who love me. I am very real in my daughter's eyes, and emotionally connected to her. If she has kids, she'll love and embrace them. I know that my healing efforts now benefit other daughters of ghost mothers, and this is very gratifying.

So, this is my ghost story, now let's start to explore yours, what it looks like, and how it's contributing to the problems you currently experience. We'll work together to come to terms with your ghost mother, and to transform your pain into visible, and exciting new ways of being in the world.

Exercise for this chapter:

Reading my ghost story may trigger emotions, or memories about your own. Take a few minutes to write down the thoughts that came up for you, without making any judgments, or feeling the need to do anything about them. Just write down your initial reactions.

I highly recommend getting a journal to use while working through the exercises in this book, as well as to record any intriguing thoughts you have as you are reading. This is also a great way to track progress, and to refer back to the changes that occur as you increase your understanding of ghost mothers. Make sure it's for your eyes only, so you feel free to express your truth. Your journal can also include drawings, quotes, and poems etc. that define the person you are becoming.

CHAPTER 2

DEFINING THE GHOST MOTHER

**Understanding the qualities that make
a mother a ghost.**

*It's not easy being a mother. If it were easy,
fathers would do it.*
 ~ *The Golden Girls*

Does Your Mother Fit the Ghost Criteria?

The first step in this journey is to look closely at the qualities that define a ghost mother, what factors contribute to the illusiveness that keeps her from being emotionally available? A ghost mother is an illusion, an apparition we desperately want to interpret as being more than it really is. She isn't fully present for her children; but is an amorphous, vague presence that exists physically, but not emotionally. What you see is not what you get. Ghost mothers come in a variety of forms, ranging from really scary to barely visible, the commonality is having very little real substance, barely enough to sustain her, and certainly not enough to share with the children she brings into the world. Being a mother requires putting your child's needs before your own, but ghost mothers have considerable difficulty doing so.

Your healing requires being clear about the issues that make your mother a ghost. I don't think this type of mother deliberately neglects her children's needs, or intends to make their lives miserable. In most cases she's doing the best she can, often not having received the nurturing she needed growing up. Identifying the illusive aspects of your mother, understanding what doesn't exist inside of her, will help you to better understand what she is, and isn't, capable of giving. The bottom line is this, a ghost mother gives the illusion of parenting, but isn't really there for you. She's not tuned into who you are or what you need; and often expects you to attend to her needs—to receive from you, rather than give to you. Many factors can contribute to this illusiveness to include: personality disorders, prolonged stress, PTSD, addictions, enabling someone else's addiction, depression, unresolved childhood issues, trauma, anxiety, physical health issues, mental illness, and in some cases being obsessively focused on other interests. What we are looking at is the essence of her presence in your life; what it feels like to be around her, what she has to give, and what she doesn't.

Let's use this as our definition: *A ghost mother is unable to unconditionally love, emotionally connect with, or successfully nurture her child.* At this point, I suspect you're wondering whether your mother meets the ghost criteria. In order to help you answer this question, I've developed three evaluation tools to help identify the extent of your mother's ghost characteristics. Since you're reading this book, there's a good chance you're aware of unresolved issues with your mother, or within yourself, and want to explore if ghost mother issues are at the core, or contributing to the difficulties you're experiencing.

To complete **quiz #1** review this list of behaviors and note which ones describe your mother's demeanor while you were growing up. If you have difficulty remembering some of these details, then answer based on how she acts in your current relationship. Don't spend too much time on each question; just go with your gut response as you move along.

⎾ **Quiz #1: Do you have a ghost mother?** ⏋

Check the characteristics that describe your mother:

1. __ Appears disinterested when you share thoughts, or feelings, with her.
2. __ Focuses more on taking care of herself than taking care of you.
3. __ Comes across as filled with anger that's often directed at you.
4. __ Makes no effort to see the world through your eyes.
5. __ Often demeans or criticizes you.
6. __ Isn't able to provide helpful advice or guidance.
7. __ Isn't there to help when you need her, even in emergencies.
8. __ Acts in ways that make you fearful of her.
9. __ Ignores your achievements, and your desires.
10. __ Is overly concerned about what others think of you.
11. __ Inappropriately discusses personal issues with you.
12. __ Expects you to take care of her emotionally.

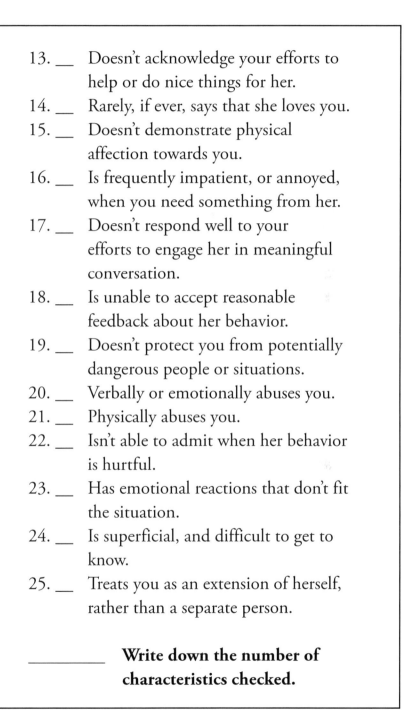

13. __ Doesn't acknowledge your efforts to help or do nice things for her.
14. __ Rarely, if ever, says that she loves you.
15. __ Doesn't demonstrate physical affection towards you.
16. __ Is frequently impatient, or annoyed, when you need something from her.
17. __ Doesn't respond well to your efforts to engage her in meaningful conversation.
18. __ Is unable to accept reasonable feedback about her behavior.
19. __ Doesn't protect you from potentially dangerous people or situations.
20. __ Verbally or emotionally abuses you.
21. __ Physically abuses you.
22. __ Isn't able to admit when her behavior is hurtful.
23. __ Has emotional reactions that don't fit the situation.
24. __ Is superficial, and difficult to get to know.
25. __ Treats you as an extension of herself, rather than a separate person.

_____ **Write down the number of characteristics checked.**

If you checked fewer than three characteristics in quiz #1, then most likely you are not dealing with a ghost mother, and in fact have a mother who did a reasonably good job of mothering. That is unless she was physically, or verbally abusive, in which case you most likely have more than three checks on your list.

In a perfect world we'd hope for no checkmarks on this list, but ghost mothers who create the depth of pain that we're exploring fall considerably short of providing adequate mothering. The more behaviors you checked, the more ghost qualities your mother has, and the more substantial the impact growing up this way has had on you. Keep in mind that some ghost mothers are completely disengaged emotionally, while some are only moderately so.

Let's continue to explore these characteristics by looking at how you feel when interacting with your mother. **Quiz #2 looks at desirable traits in a mother, and quiz #3 looks at undesirable traits.** Work through both of the quizzes below, and then we'll discuss the valuable information this process provides. Answer the questions quickly, without thinking too much about your responses.

Quiz #2: What does it feel like to be with your mother?
(Desirable traits)

Check all that apply.

1. __ I feel that I'm special to her.
2. __ I feel loved by her.
3. __ She appreciates what I do for her.
4. __ I feel that she understands me.
5. __ I feel she's interested in my dreams, and what's important to me.
6. __ I feel motivated when I'm with her to be the best I can be.
7. __ I feel listened to and understood.
8. __ I want to share my ideas, and feelings with her.
9. __ I know I can count on her, especially during difficult times.
10. __ I seek her advice and find it helpful.
11. __ I feel that she respects me.
12. __ I see her as my advocate in life.
13. __ She genuinely cares about my health and well-being.
14. __ I think about her fondly when we aren't together.

_____ **Write down the number checked.**

Quiz #2 looks at the positive feelings you experience when spending time with your mother, or thinking about her. On this quiz, the more checks the better. Even a mother who scored poorly on quiz #1 may have positive attributes that show up on this quiz. Now, complete quiz #3, which identifies undesirable ghost-traits in a mother.

Quiz #3: What does it feel like to be with your mother?
(Undesirable traits)

Check all that apply.

1. __ I often feel confused about what she wants from me.
2. __ I don't think she's interested in what I say or feel.
3. __ When we interact, she wants to control the conversation.
4. __ I frequently don't know what to say to her.
5. __ I'm tired of being criticized or ignored, by her.
6. __ She really doesn't know me very well.
7. __ I think she frequently lies to me.
8. __ I feel judged by her.
9. __ It's frustrating to try to communicate with her.
10. __ I feel sad when I'm with her.
11. __ I feel angry when I'm with her.
12. __ I feel I want more from her than I'm getting.
13. __ Sometimes I deliberately avoid contact with her.
14. __ Sometimes I fantasize about doing things to hurt her.

_____ **Write down the number checked.**

Quiz #3 looks at the negative qualities exhibited by your mother in your relationship; did you check three or more? If so, there's a good chance you are dealing with a ghost mother, and in most cases the characteristics checked in the first quiz will be consistent with the negative feelings you experience when dealing with her. For example, if you checked question #11 on quiz 3, *I feel angry when I'm with her*, then perhaps you also checked question #4 on quiz #1, *Makes no effort to see the world through your eyes.*

These quizzes were developed to help you identify ghost traits in your mother, and in your relationship with her. The more qualities you checked in quizzes 1 and 3, the more illusive your mother is, and the more problematic your relationship with her is likely to be. Go back and see if there are repeated patterns to the qualities you identified. For example, perhaps you'll see several instances of being ignored by your mother, feeling angry towards her, or noticing that she wasn't there when you needed her. Now that you've worked through this information, I don't recommend confronting her about what you learned in looking at her from this perspective. The insights you've just acquired are best discussed with a therapist, friend, or someone other than your mother. Blaming her gets you nowhere, and she's unlikely to understand, or accept responsibility for the deficits in her mothering. If she *did* have this level of insight, and capacity for self-reflection, these problems would probably not exist in the first place.

For most women, there's a sense of relief in developing clarity about these ghost issues. The personal stories shared in this book, and explanations about the impact of growing up with a ghost mother will paint an even clearer picture of the long-term effects of being raised by a ghost. Women often have some issues with their mothers, even more so at particular times in their development, such as adolescence, but these aren't the issues addressed in this book. What we're talking about are ongoing issues of lack, negligent mothers, mothers unable to connect with or guide us, mothers that are cruel or self-centered, abusive mothers who lash out. These are mother-daughter issues that do a considerable amount of damage to our psyche, and sense of self. Perhaps what you've suspected has now been confirmed; you've been trying to get love and nurturing from a mother who isn't able to provide these compassionate qualities.

Telling Ghost Stories

Isn't it reasonable to expect to receive love and nurturing from our own mother? It certainly is, but what we need and deserve is not always what we get, and surely not when it comes to dealing with a ghost mother. This type of illusive mother comes in a variety of forms, based on a number of factors to include her personality, childhood, and the core cause of her issues. Now it's time to gather 'round the fire to hear some poignant stories from five women who grew up with a ghost mother. This information will help clarify the various presentations a ghost mother can take, and the pain that emerges in being on the receiving end of her version of mothering.

Susan describes her ghost mother:

My mother has always been mean and manipulative to get what she wants; her needs have always superseded mine. I became the mother to my mother at an early age, valued only for what I did for her, not for who I was. I took her on trips, bought her things I knew she liked, cooked her special food, took her to dinner and cultural events; but none of this made any difference, it was never enough. Like fog, she enveloped me, blurred and distorted my vision for way too many years; I became invisible. When my father died, the buffer no longer existed, and everything that was wrong in the relationship between my mother and me reached a crescendo. She sees herself as a victim of everyone, everything, in every situation. No one, absolutely NO ONE has it as bad as she does . . . last summer she said to me, right after I had been in the hospital with a kidney stone, "My kidney stone was worse than yours." One of her physical therapists told her in front of me, "You remind me of Eeyore;" she did not understand what he was talking about.

Every interaction with her deteriorates to bad feelings, exasperation, anger, and total frustration. She can push my buttons within seconds. There's always a considerable amount of drama in dealing with my mother. She'll call in a panic and ask, "Are you still alive?" When I go out of town she asks, "What are you going to do if I die while you are gone, have you faxed my funeral plans to your brother?" She is envious and jealous of many of the things that I do; she actually competes with me in many ways. In conversations, she constantly interrupts and tries to 'trump' anything that I say.

Jody portrays her mother in a compelling way:

Mom's verbal attacks about the badness of my character were so piercing that the effect today is I walk around with this odd self-belief that I'm condemned, shameful and bad. She would give me mean glances, saying, "Don't feel so good about yourself, I hate you." She always wanted me to be afraid of her, the threats were constant; she kept a wooden spoon on my dresser, and constantly raged at me. She put a scary skull in my room, and wouldn't allow me to remove it. When I told her that screaming at me hurt my feelings, she said, "Oh well, get over it." There was no consideration of me, or how I felt, at all.

Mom's idea of sharing her feelings is to do or say something that makes me feel the same way she's feeling, she feels bad so she wants me to feel the same way; she accomplishes this by attacking, or condemning me. When I was growing up, she would be sure, when no one was around to hear or see what she was doing, to make statements to show that she didn't love me. She did this by threatening to reject me, and to stop taking care of me, making comments to include, "I thought about aborting you." "I don't care about you, get out of my face."

Lynne's mother didn't even notice when she walked out the door:

I grew up in a home where I didn't receive compassion, empathy, or validation for my emotions. She was clueless to all my activities including my school performance. My dad went to open house school night without her. It was subtle emotional torture for me, so I ran away from home every day (when I was three years old), heading out the door to visit our neighbor, with my mini-broom and dustpan in hand. How interesting that I needed to prove my self-worth by offering to clean her home, instead of just visiting.

My mother didn't try to stop me; she laughed, and didn't even ask where I was going, or why. Growing up with my mother was like hearing the pilot of an airplane say, "Go ahead and move about the cabin freely." My childhood felt free and totally ungrounded. Free to make my own choices because it was one less thing my mother had to deal with, and ungrounded because trust and emotional comfort was never offered.

Michelle describes the literal pain of growing up with her mother:

Sometimes when I talk to my mom she pretends to fall asleep, as if what I have to say is boring, or of no importance to her. As a teenager, I wasn't allowed to lock the bathroom door. My mom would often come in; as I saw the doorknob turn I would quickly pull the curtain around the tub. She'd enter the bathroom annoyed with me, saying, "You think you're too good, too perfect, for anyone to see you naked." This made me feel confused and angry with her. She would read my diary, and then mock me for the inner feelings that I'd written down. She always wanted a taste of the finer things in life, and would stare at people when we visited the city, envying their fur coats, jewelry, and so on. So she would often take me, and my younger sister, to an urban area to shop for nicer clothes. We had to be decked out in the best of the best; I think it was to make her look better in the eyes of others that we were dressed to the hilt.

From ages 4-6 my mother severely abused me. To this day, I have not told anyone about what she did. But, I clearly remember what she did, and where it occurred. I wanted to get help, but she told me this is what was best for me. She told me to be a good girl, and not to scream. The abuse was done in private, and my father was never around when it took place. I suppose that was part of her plan.

Tanya's mother didn't protect her:

My mother has always tried to control me, push me around, and blame me for things I had nothing to do with. According to her, she was always right and I was always wrong. She acted coldly towards me, lacked empathy, and had no real concern for what happened to me. My father sexually abused me as a teenager. When I told my mother he was molesting me, she yelled and screamed at me, accused me of lying, and did nothing to stop him.

She displayed no concern for me, ever, but I would keep going back to get what I needed from my mother. I've been bewildered and angered by my mother's behavior for years. There are a number of times she has contradicted herself, even in the same sentence. When I had surgery, after being diagnosed with cancer, she insisted I attend her birthday party; a full day's drive through the mountains, when I was under doctor's orders not to travel, at all. She wanted me there, my life-threatening illness, surgery, healing—none of it mattered to her at all.

The recurring themes in these stories define ghost mothers, quite clearly, as a woman unable to be compassionate, or empathic due to her own insecurity, emptiness, and emotional immaturity. This type of mother has no boundaries, is controlling, insecure, and often critical, or demeaning. Your experience with a ghost mother may have been similar, or very different, but with the same themes of inadequate love, concern or protection. A good, or even adequate, mother raises a child who emerges with a sense of self, knowing she is loveable because she has known real love. A mother with a deep sense of inadequacy cannot do this. If you now see, or suspect, that your mother is a ghost, I encourage you to try to view this from a positive perspective because you are now beginning to understand the core cause of what isn't working in your life. Armed with this knowledge you can do something about it. You are in the right place, at the right time, because I'm going to take you by the hand, explain the consequences of this pain to you, and show you how to use this experience as an opportunity for powerful transformation.

The Excuses We Make, the Lies We Tell Ourselves

A primary issue that haunted me in my healing journey was this, why did I chase my ghost mother for so long? In hindsight it doesn't make much sense that I continued to hope my mother would suddenly start to interact in a more caring manner, and yet, I remained hopeful, even when things continued to get worse, instead of better. It seemed like the colder and crueler, she acted towards me, the more determined I became to reverse this process, to somehow gain her love. Against all odds, I continued to believe this wasn't my real mother I was dealing with, that the nurturing woman I needed would surely emerge. I thought that I just needed to be patient and keep trying. Most women who are raised by a ghost feel this way, that we are the ones who need to figure out the key to unlocking our mother's love for us. The reasons we hang on so tightly to the desire for a nurturing mother are important to understand. Some of these explanations may apply to you more than others:

- **The longing for a nurturing mother.** The deep need for a mother who will guide, love and protect us is a basic, primitive instinct. When we're young, we need her to survive, and even when she's not doing her job, our desire to be more deeply connected with her remains strong.

- **Shame that our mother treats us in such a disinterested manner.** There is a considerable amount of difficulty in accepting her limitations because of the belief that this reflects poorly on us, that we are un-deserving of better treatment.

- **Disbelief that this is all there is.** We don't want things to be this way between us, so we do everything possible to convince ourselves it just isn't true.

- **Fears we will be just like her.** The more we allow ourselves to admit she falls short of what we need, the more we may see her flaws and limitations in our own behavior. If we judge her critically, we may need to admit our own shortcomings as well.

- **Not wanting to let go of the possibility that things will improve.** Wanting so desperately to have a fully functioning mother makes it difficult to part with the possibility, however remote, that this situation will get better.

- **Thinking this is our fault; that we are to blame for her poor parenting.** We worry that perhaps we aren't loveable; that we are doing something wrong, or haven't yet figured out the right words to express what we need from her.

It's common to resist coming to terms with the painful reality that a ghost mother will remain an illusion in our life, that it's unlikely she will ever make positive changes, or behave in more nurturing ways. Denying this reality may seem more comfortable than having to face the truth. The painful fact that our mother is not providing what we need is extremely difficult to accept. As the daughter of a ghost we tend to blame ourselves, making excuses for her behavior, hanging onto a fragile sense of hope, believing she will one day respond to us differently.

Susan shared some interesting thoughts in this regard: *I am mad at myself for hanging onto false hope, and magical thinking. I have ignored my needs while yearning for acceptance from a mother who would put her arms around me, and tell me how much she loves me.*

I frequently felt like a dog in dealing with my mother, any crumb she threw to me I devoured, while hoping for more. I think this happens because we are so desperate for loving interactions with her. When we receive even a tiny aspect of this, we not only relish the moment, we allow it to create a strong sense of hope that more will follow. In response to any kindness from her, we respond with optimistic thoughts such as: *If she does this for me occasionally, why can't it happen more often? I must have finally done something right; I need to figure out what it was, so I can do it again.* Behavior therapists could have a field day with this concept, the idea of rats frantically searching for a small piece of cheese—because they received it once in a blue moon. It's a brutal comparison, but unfortunately it's true; we lie to ourselves, repeatedly, in order to avoid the painful reality that what we are getting from our ghost mother is all she has to give.

What drives our denial makes sense, but by surrounding ourselves in this illusion it's easy to get stuck in our ghost mother's reality. It's when we recognize the truth for what it is; that we can stop chasing what isn't there. Trying to deny the reality of having an illusive mother doesn't serve us at all.

Chasing an Illusive Mother, How Her Problems Become Your Pain

The desire to be nurtured by your mother is natural, normal and healthy. To want to be seen as special in her eyes, delighted over, lovingly guided through the early years of life. It's not your longing, or your belief that a mother's role is to assist her child in feeling loved, needed, and protected that is the problem. The problem is that she's a ghost, making it impossible for her to perform successfully in the role of a real mother. The result is that her problems become your pain.

Once during a heated argument with my mother, I expressed my opinion that I'd been through numerous hellish times with her, and asked what positive experiences she thought she'd provided to me. I couldn't think of any, but imagined she would have a different view. She paused and said, "Well, there must be something." The fact that she couldn't identify any motherly accomplishments stunned me, and helped me realize she simply didn't see this as her role. She was floating in a very different reality, one in which she expected me to focus on her needs. What I needed from her really wasn't important. Obviously, I felt differently, and I'm sure you do too.

Let's look now at the painful issues that emerge when a ghost mother raises you. How do these ghost issues impact you? Why does this lack of mothering haunt you so deeply, and for so long?

Listed below are some of the emotions women experience as the result of being inadequately mothered:

Ashamed

Unworthy

Empty

Lost

Angry

Sad

Lonely

Fearful

Confused

Deprived

Disillusioned

Rejected

Heartbroken

As a result of not receiving love, and the ongoing struggle to get what you need from your mother, being raised by a ghost has the overall effect of creating three critical issues that need to be recognized, and dealt with.

The three issues are:

1. **The limited development of a sense of self, and a deep sense of un-worthiness.**

   It's quite difficult to get to know, or like yourself, when you aren't reflected back positively by a primary role model. This is further compounded by the fear that your mother remains at a distance because you don't measure up, and often develops into the belief that there's something fundamentally wrong with you.

2. **Uncertainty about what love, and normal relationships look like.**

When we don't know what is reasonable to expect from others, the result is often to ignore, or to be unable to identify our own needs. In addition, we don't feel entitled to ask for what we need from others, and are reluctant to trust anyone, including ourselves.

3. **Difficulty defining our place, value, and importance in the world.**

With so much energy directed towards getting our basic needs met, we often grow up, and go into the real world poorly prepared to live, and love. We don't know our strengths, question our value, and feel a deep sense of emptiness and abandonment. It's like setting off on a journey without a road map, and not knowing your destination.

In growing up with a ghost mother, we frequently contort ourselves in our efforts to connect with, and get what we need from her. It's essential to recognize that she's found ways to cope that work for her; you are the one who is left hurting. A ghost mother isn't fully present, and doesn't know how to be more emotionally connected; she has no idea that she's a ghost. We need our ghost mother to care for us, but she doesn't have what we need . . . it's as simple, and as painful as that. This isn't a blame game, your mother did the best she could with what she had to work with, but the reality is that if she'd had to apply for this job, she wouldn't have gotten it.

Lack of mothering leaves you with a sense that something within you is missing. You know the situation just isn't right; you seek a deeper, richer happier life, but don't know how to find it. Half the battle is to recognize the enemy you are fighting. In this case it's not actually your mother, it's what she wasn't able to provide, and the devastating impact this has had on you. Now that we've defined the qualities that make a mother a ghost, in the next chapter we're going to explore a psychological disorder that creates problems that may describe your type of ghost mother.

Exercise for this chapter:

Dealing with ghost mother issues can be emotionally overwhelming. This simple exercise increases your ability to easily use your breath to decrease anxiety, and quiet your thoughts by quickly introducing calming energy into your body; think of it as a natural tranquilizer that's always available to you. Don't be put off by the detailed directions; all you need to do is breath through one nostril, and then the other.

Alternate Nostril Breathing:

Sit down and close your eyes.
Press your thumb to close your right nostril.
Inhale slowly through the left nostril, while slowly counting to 4.
Pause for a second.
Close your left nostril with the ring finger, and exhale slowly through the right nostril, counting to 8.
Now inhale through the right nostril, while counting to 4.
Pause for a second.
Close the right nostril with your thumb.
Breathe out through your left nostril to the count of 8.
This is one round, continue for three rounds.

CHAPTER 3

A VERY SCARY KIND OF GHOST MOTHER

Is your mother self-absorbed to the point of being a narcissist?

But enough about me, let's talk about you . . .
what do YOU think of me?
~ The Movie, Beaches

Is Your Ghost Mother a Narcissist?

Ghost mothers are self-absorbed for a variety of reasons, sometimes it's possible to identify what these issues are, and other times the reasons remain a mystery. I gained considerable insight into my situation when I came to understand that my mother sees the world through the distorted lens of a mental health disorder known as *Narcissistic Personality Disorder (NPD)*. Although I had learned about this disorder in my training, it took many years before I understood that this was the core cause of her problems, and the problems between us. If your relationship with your mother is an exceedingly difficult one, it's worth learning more about NPD, and how it manifests in the mother-daughter relationship. In my efforts to learn more about narcissism I participated in a class facilitated by Patricia E. Patton, PH.D, an expert who lectures on this subject in southern California. She agreed to be interviewed for this book and her insights are interspersed throughout this chapter.

What I've learned is that a narcissistic mother usually has some, or all, of the following characteristics:

- **Mood swings**
- **Demanding**
- **Lives in her own world**
- **Easily offended**
- **Manipulative**
- **Controlling**
- **Envious**
- **Rejecting**
- **Blaming**

In many ways, the narcissistic mother is the epitome of a ghost mother. She is selfish and emotionally disconnected, to the point of viewing her children as an extension of herself, and available to do her bidding. In a complete role reversal, a mother with this disorder expects her daughter to reflect back what a wonderful person she is in order to meet her own emotional needs. This pathological self-doubt creates a mother who takes from her children, and is unable to give in return. As Dr. Patton comments, *Female narcissists may view their children as sources of narcissistic supply, and demand unrealistic attention from them, even throughout their adult lives.*

Let's explore the traits that define this disorder, and what it feels like to interact with a mother who is a narcissist, to determine if this explains the dynamics of your experience with a ghost mother. This type of mother is uniquely qualified to make you feel inadequate because no matter how hard you try to please her, it's never going to be enough to provide the self-esteem that she doesn't have. When I initially began to explore the possibility that my mother could have a mental health issue, I thought depression might explain her troubled mood, and behavior, but there were too many problems in our relationship that weren't consistent with depression. Feelings of sadness were part of the problem, but didn't explain it fully.

As I learned more about NPD, I was surprised at how well this diagnosis described my ghost mother, and my interactions with her. I was troubled by this reality, but at the same time felt a sense of relief because the mystery of my mother was starting to be revealed. It explained a great deal, but at the same time it was difficult to comprehend the extent of the self-absorbed behaviors that are the hallmark of this disorder. So, I did considerable research, trying to understand, hoping there was another explanation that wasn't so extreme, so unlikely to ever improve. This was a painful process, but one that provided the information I needed to finally understand her, and the problems between us. Even with the clarity I gained, I did not want to see my own mother in this light, did not want to know that she had such substantial deficits.

This knowledge finally explained why my ongoing efforts to make a positive emotional connection with her were never successful. It dramatically shifted my view of her, my understanding of our relationship, and illuminated the fact that I wasn't the problem after all. As part of my healing I wrote a letter to her in 2003, describing how I now viewed the problems between us. I didn't send this letter since the intention of doing this was therapeutic, to help sort out the new perspective I was struggling to understand, and come to terms with. This is the letter that I wrote:

Dear Mom,

It feels like I've spent my entire life trying to get you to love me. I've longed for your caring, concern and support more than you'll ever know. I've wanted to believe that if I finally did, or said, the right thing, that if I continued to hang in there with you, you'd become the loving mother I needed. This hope has been shattered; I'm now forced to accept the severity of your problems, and in doing so the pieces of this bizarre puzzle have begun to come together.

The reality that you manage your life by using others has provided insight into many aspects of our relationship that I didn't understand before. Yet, I don't want to accept any of this. How can my Mommy, who I've needed so desperately, not be able to provide any nurturing to me? How can she not be able to love, or care about me? How can the woman who gave birth to me, end up using me for her own benefit? There are still far more questions than answers as I struggle to comprehend the reality of the problem we are dealing with.

I've given far more to you than I've ever given myself; I've tried to fix your problems instead of my own. I can't believe that I've put up with this for so long, that I've worked so hard to improve a hopeless situation, that I continued trying when there were no signs of hope. Deep inside I know it was because I wanted so much to please you, to make you happy, so that I could experience your love. I've longed to have what other mothers and daughters share, for you to be the person I can turn to, who loves me no matter what.

In return I've received the constant message that what I give is never enough. I now understand that you are trying to fill a deep emptiness inside of you, and no one else can do that for you. I wake up filled with a deep longing for what will never be. I wish so much that you could be a happy, and fulfilled person. I wish for so many things that will never be. On particularly bad days, it feels like we're drowning together in the ocean. I picture that you're clinging to me, and that if we stay in this position we'll both go under. This forces me to not only let go of you, but to have to push you away, for my own survival.

When I picture doing this, the water starts to swirl dangerously around my head, and as I consider letting myself sink into its murky depth, I realize that perhaps you've given me something after all. Perhaps, although it wasn't your intention, you've shown me how to swim. Perhaps I've learned that loving and taking care of myself is the only way to get safely to shore. I'm discovering a depth inside of me that I hadn't known existed.

I could have drowned while clinging to you; instead I found the will to keep swimming, and *the courage to face the pain. When I became so discouraged that I was willing to accept whatever came next, the world opened itself to me. I've come to see myself as a strong and determined swimmer, learned to trust my intuition, and to know that what I feel inside is very real. Now, I'm alive and free, and I'm not drowning anymore . . .*

Not only does the daughter of a narcissist miss out on appropriate mothering, we are taught to take care of others at our own expense. In popular culture, a narcissist is seen as having a huge ego, and moving confidently through the world, however, this mask of superiority is just that, a mask covering up the fact that this confidence, and self-esteem, doesn't really exist. "While their sense of superiority may seem perfectly intact, it requires constant bolstering," explains psychologist Terri Apter in her book, **Difficult Mothers.**

A mother with an excessive amount of narcissism attempts to cope on a very primitive level; one in which she depends on others to boost her fragile sense of self, and who better to take on this role than a child she has complete control over? The constant need for validation, approval, and attention from others is known as *narcissistic supply*, and it seems to become a drug to someone with this disorder. With it, she feels better; without it, she rages at the people who aren't providing it to her. This dynamic is further complicated by the fact that there is such significant role reversal, and that, behind closed doors, the narcissistic mother acts much differently than she does in public.

The word narcissism was derived from a Greek myth about a handsome young man named Narcissus, much sought after by the nymphs in the woods, including one who was particularly infatuated with him named Echo. He cruelly rebuffed her; he rebuffed all the nymphs who were attracted to him. So strong was his vanity that when he caught sight of his own reflection in a pond, he couldn't take his eyes off it. He tried to embrace, and kiss, his own image as it reflected in the water, but when he reached out to touch the person he saw, he was unable to do so. The reflection was merely an image, one that became even more distorted by the ripples created when he touched the water. While impressed with his outside presentation, inside he was tortured by this obsession with himself.

There are numerous versions of how this story ends, including Narcissus killing himself, drowning, or being killed by the Gods. This is a fascinating myth, not only does the story end badly due to Narcissus' obsession with his physical appearance, but it also highlights how tormented he felt inside, initially by not finding anyone who met his high standards, and then by becoming so focused on his reflection that he could think of nothing else. He was unable to connect with others, and couldn't connect with himself—which in simple terms is the sad plight of the narcissist. It's this story, and pattern of self-defeating behavior, that was embraced by the mental health profession, and woven into a description of the traits that officially labels someone as a narcissist.

These traits include:

- An **exaggerated sense of self-importance**, to the point of lying about achievements.
- **Demands adulation and attention** from others.
- **A sense of entitlement**, i.e. demands that others comply with her demands.
- **Feels uniquely special**, and expects others to treat her as such.
- **Exploits others** to get what she wants.
- **Becomes easily enraged** when confronted by others.
- Is unable to feel what others may be feeling, i.e. has **no empathy.**
- An **arrogant, or haughty** demeanor.
- **Envies others**, and believes others envy her.

When someone exhibits **five** or more of these traits on a consistent basis, according to the definitive listing of mental health disorders developed by the American Psychiatric Association, the person meets the criteria to be diagnosed as having Narcissistic Personality Disorder (NPD). In case you're wondering, the term "personality disorders" describes maladaptive behaviors, and ways of viewing the world, that usually develop in adolescence, or early adulthood. If this disorder seems to describe your mother, it's important to know that this is a pervasive way of coping with deep feelings of inadequacy, and one that is rarely amenable to treatment.

Dr. Patton further explains the characteristics that identify a narcissist:

Pathological envy, inability to hold other people's perspectives in mind, not learning from the mistakes they make with others, poor reality-testing skills; which can make them "legends in their own minds." Their worldview is a black-and-white, all-or-nothing dichotomy, in which others are totally "for" or "against" them. This leads to feelings of rejection when others even slightly disagree with them—and in turn, the narcissist usually rejects them in a brutally painful way.

These patterns of behavior become evident in a relationship over time, and a narcissist is gifted in her ability to present as charming to others, a fact that makes her children—who know the truth about the interactions at home—feel confused, frustrated and angry. This is in many ways similar to an alcoholic mother, who acts fine while in the company of others, but at home becomes inebriated, and acts quite differently.

What Your Narcissistic Mother Wants to Get From You

When I was nineteen, I was living with my mother, but spent a week in Michigan hanging out with a friend. One night we partied much too hard. This was a time in my life when I was using drugs and alcohol to numb the pain I was feeling, but didn't know how to deal with, as I grieved my father's death, and attempted to understand the worsening problems with my mother.

I consumed several brownies that were laced with marijuana, at the same time that I drank a large amount of red wine. At first I liked how I felt, and then I got dizzy, and began having hallucinations in which the same scene kept happening over, and over again. Time became completely so distorted that I didn't know what was real, and what was repeating. I was terrified; so the guy I was staying with called an ambulance. I went to the hospital where I was medically monitored while I came down from this frightening high for the next twelve hours.

Fortunately, I didn't suffer any permanent damage from my drug overdose, although I felt lousy for the remainder of my vacation. I had the presence of mind when I checked out of the hospital to pay the bill so that my mother would have no knowledge of this incident. But a few days later a statement was sent (in my name) to the house, and she opened it. I saw the bill on her desk, and dreaded what might come next. She angrily asked me what had happened, but her only response when I told her was, "I hope you don't think I'm going to pay for this."

She expressed no concern about what had happened, how I was feeling, or whether there were any medical ramifications. She didn't even mention the obvious question, why was I abusing drugs in the first place? She didn't seem to care; her only concern was that her daughter might have run up a hospital bill that she would have to pay. When she responded in this manner, when she revealed that her only concern about this incident was the balance in her checkbook, I felt completely discounted, invisible, and uncared for.

The disorder of narcissism clearly warps a person's view of the world, and her perspective as a mother. For my mother to respond to this disturbing incident with such coldness, concerned only about the impact on her, is a devastating example of how the world looks to a narcissist, and how this disorder keeps her from being emotionally connected to others.

Two of the women who have previously shared their stories have also recognized that narcissism is the core cause of the problems with their ghost mother.

Lynne describes what it was like to grow up with her narcissistic mother:

I grew up in a world where my thoughts and feelings didn't matter to anyone, least of all my mother. I was a burden for having a need. A perfect example of this still haunts me, getting teased incessantly by our neighbor's daughter for wearing dresses that were too big, and down to my ankles. My mother didn't notice, or care, how unhappy this teasing made me. We were rich; there was no financial reason for me to be dressed like this.

When I tried to talk to her, she was disinterested and vacant, and disappeared within herself to the point of having a blank, flinty stare on her face, as though she had to tolerate listening to something she didn't choose to be involved with. If I tried to talk about myself, it was never long before she interrupted, and brought the conversation back to herself. My mother can't have a normal conversation; she does monologues, never engaging in give and take. When we're alone, she bullies or criticizes me, but in a room full of people she compliments me on something that she insists I inherited from her! I have never experienced unconditional love, except from my children. I grew up without maternal support, and have no true connection with my mother; she is a narcissist who has never added any value to my life. I don't know the exact age when I completely gave up on relying on my mother for safety or trust, but I can remember all the events that led up to this decision.

Jody describes the behavior of her self-absorbed, mean mother:

Mom has never taken responsibility for her emotions, and has never respected my feelings at all. I learned at a young age that my job was to make mom feel good about herself, or she would come at me with personal attacks. One day after school, I made myself a veggie taco, and was putting it in the microwave when she walked in and noticed I wasn't frying up any ground beef. I told mom the truth, "I didn't make this for you, it's for me and I only like veggies." Her response was completely off the topic, "Don't have kids, they ruin your life." Then she added, "You don't love me enough." Then for no apparent reason, she threatened suicide by saying, "If I don't wake up in the morning, it's all your fault."

Mom completely "lost it" because I made a snack for myself, and didn't include her. Because of how she's treated me over the years, I've never felt okay just being myself, and have always felt I needed to change into someone very different. She likes to brag about her amazing brilliance, and most conversations are dominated by her talking about how the people she works with are inept idiots. She was clearly jealous of me growing up, she would get angry when I wore a bikini, shouting at me, "I could never look that good." So now I wasn't supposed to wear a bikini because it made her feel bad about herself? When I wanted hugs from her she would look at me and say, "You always want something from me." I was made to feel like a burden to want anything from her.

These stories show the frustration, and confusion in trying to understand why efforts to please a narcissistic mother continually fail, as well as the eventual acceptance that a mother with this disorder has very little to give, that she can't be counted on, trusted, or expected to be nurturing or empathic.

Let's look further at the specific ways narcissism impacts a mother's ability to parent, keeping in mind that the extent of self-absorption that characterizes this disorder varies widely. My mother has all the traits of NPD; many ghost mothers will exhibit this disturbing behavior in more moderate ways. Your mother may only have one of the narcissistic traits previously listed, so her difficult behavior will not be as extreme. But having any of these traits will contribute to her emotional unavailability as a mother, and these issues of self-absorption will negatively impact her ability to be nurturing, and empathic.

The problems that develop in dealing with a narcissistic mother are similar to the patterns that develop in dealing with any type of ghost mother, but there are some unique qualities to include:

- **It feels like you're an extension of her.**
- **You're expected to let her know what a wonderful person she is.**
- **Nothing you do pleases her, or is good enough in her eyes.**
- **Focusing on your needs elicits an angry response from her.**
- **She's manipulative to get what she wants from you.**
- **Her behaviors, and mood are unpredictable.**
- **She minimizes any concerns you try to discuss with her.**

Having to attend to my mother's needs meant that I was constantly tuned into anticipating what she wanted from me, and how to respond in ways that avoided an angry tongue-lashing. I've come to understand that this dynamic occurs because of the insecure feelings a narcissist *projects* onto others—a psychological term used to describe this behavior. Dumping her difficult feelings onto you may help your mother feel better, but you end up wondering what you did to deserve such treatment. There's no room in a relationship with a narcissist for your separate identity to emerge, no opportunity to identify or focus on your needs; the relationship is all about pleasing her.

In the book **Disarming the Narcissist**, Wendy T. Behary, LCSW discusses the differences between female and male narcissists, clarifying that for the female narcissist, the *"Resounding and self-affirming mantra is, 'You owe me'."* I think this point captures the very essence of a narcissistic mother; when I came across this information it sounded eerily familiar. A narcissistic mother has to depend on others to feel okay about herself, but at the same time she is angry about the degree of her dependence.

> **Lynne** captures the essence of what it feels like to constantly feel indebted, and in service, to a narcissistic mother: *Being around her is like being a puppet on strings.*

Not only is this a huge burden for the daughter of a narcissist, it also means that this type of ghost mother isn't able to reflect back our positive qualities, help us figure out our feelings, or what's important to us, because she's unable to provide this essential mirroring that most mothers are capable of. Now that I've gotten distance from dealing with this disorder in my mother, I've come to better understand the peculiar dynamics of growing up this way. I see that we were two women with strikingly different agendas. I was a child who needed love, attention and support; she was a needy, wounded woman who was challenged to meet her own emotional needs.

The Power Struggle That Doesn't End, Until You End It

In attempting to deal with the challenges presented by my narcissist mother, I tried to change her, while at the same time trying to change myself to behave in ways that were more pleasing to her. For a time, I thought I had this all figured out. If I could find ways to please her, then she'd be happy, and give me the love, attention, and approval I needed. What could possibly go wrong with this plan?

It took many years to figure out this was a plan doomed to failure, that my well-intentioned efforts couldn't succeed—but that didn't stop me from trying. To make the situation even more challenging, when my mother wasn't trying to be the center of attention, she became depressed. I never knew what to make of this, but it was troubling to have her mood change so dramatically, and without notice. One minute she was telling me how wonderful she was, and the next minute she was taking me in her confidence, telling me how awful her life was, that she had nothing.

> Dr. Patton has also noticed this pattern in NPD: *They may seek therapy when they are depressed. However, they only want relief from their depression, rather than insight into its underlying causes, as related to their personality disorder.*

I now understand this is part of the behavior pattern of a narcissist, when she feels that she's getting enough narcissistic supply, she's on top of the world, but when it's not enough, she reverts to the feelings that haunt her, the sense of emptiness and sadness. For much of my life this erratic maternal pattern made me feel crazy, and it was difficult to try to anticipate which side of her I'd have to deal with next. A narcissist is driven by ego, demands that she get her needs met by others, and is only able to validate herself through external sources.

For several decades, I tried to improve the situation with my mother by letting her know what I needed from her, and acting towards her in loving ways that I hoped would be reciprocated. I kept thinking if she understood how I needed her to be different, then her motherly instincts would kick in to help her respond positively to me. When this approach didn't work, it made me feel lonely and powerless in my relationship with her. It also made me feel that I wasn't very loveable, and that my needs weren't important.

The dynamics we've been exploring are similar to being raised by any type of ghost mother, the family appears normal to outsiders, but what's really happening is that the kids are trying to meet the mother's needs, rather than being nurtured, and taken care of. A narcissistic mother represents ghost mothering in the extreme, because the mother doesn't feel responsible for her child, and instead uses her role to get her own needs met. I finally had to face the painful realization that my mother wasn't there for me, never had been, and never would be. I recognized that she was a ghost, holding out the promise of being what I needed, but never delivering.

I was forced to accept that I was holding onto my hope for who I wanted her to be, while completely losing myself in the process. I so wanted to believe the illusion, the promise of better things to come. I did not want to accept the reality that she was manipulating me to get her own needs met, and even when I came to understand the disorder of narcissism, I still kept hoping it wasn't true.

The extent of the difficulties experienced in being raised this way depend on how narcissistic your mother is, but the existence of any of these traits in a mother can make growing up a painful journey to navigate, and one that you most likely will need help in healing from. In addition to not being nurtured or adequately mothered, the daughter of a narcissist needs to overcome being used, and abused by her own mother. It's also a painful reality that narcissists get worse as they age.

> Dr. Patton summarizes this well: *As female narcissists age, and their physical beauty changes, they may have great difficulties adapting their self-image to their changing bodies. They may not have developed other talents, or their intelligence, due to this over-emphasis on beauty, and feel an increased sense of worthlessness.*

In an article in "O" magazine, psychologist Martha Beck came up with a solution to dealing with a narcissist that I think makes a great deal of sense. In describing the dynamics of this difficult relationship, she compared it to being involved in an intense game of tug-of-war, with the narcissist on one end of the rope, and you on the other. "Drop the rope," she advised. I agree with this response; this is the only way out, the only way to end the struggle. When I finally dropped the rope with my mother, it brought a tremendous sense of relief. It was also very sad because without this constant effort to get what I needed from her, there wasn't much left between us. It turns out our relationship *was* the chasing, the struggle, and the tug-of war between us. Without it, there was not much of anything to build a relationship on.

Ghost mothers who possess only some narcissistic traits may participate in therapy, or otherwise make some adjustments in behavior, but a mother with NPD usually does not have the ability to make positive changes. Unfortunately, the struggle with a narcissistic mother brings primarily pain, and frustration; this is chasing a ghost you can't catch. She doesn't exist, except in your mind, she is an illusive ghost that can't give you what you need; sadly she doesn't have it to give.

I've gone into a significant amount of detail about narcissistic mothers because this is the type I'm most familiar with, both personally and professionally. For many women this is new information. A mother with this disorder captures the phenomenon of a ghost mother in its most vivid form. Keep in mind what you've learned so far about ghost mothers as we continue to explore the dynamics of growing up with this way, no matter what has caused her to be an illusive figure in your life. If the critical relationship with your mother isn't working, for whatever reason, the pain experienced, and the steps to healing, are the same. The next step in our journey is to increase your understanding of why the pain of a ghost mother hurts so much, and why it lingers for so long.

Exercise for this chapter:

If this chapter brought up anxiety in thinking about a mother with these qualities, take time now to do this exercise. Close your eyes and picture your mother, now shift the image to seeing her as a ghost, or as a child—it's up to you. Now adjust the picture so that she slowly begins to shrink.

Now add yourself to the picture, since she's so small you are looking down at her. Keep adjusting this image, so that she continues to diminish in size, and scariness. This new viewpoint decreases her power, and increases yours. Return to this image every time it's helpful to view your ghost mother from a different perspective. Get creative, inject a bit of humor, this can actually be fun, and is very effective.

Chapter 4

Haunted by the Past

Understanding why you are still haunted by mother issues.

Do not dwell on those who let you down, cherish those who hold you up.

- Jillian Michaels

The Much-Needed Mothering You Missed Out On

Being raised by a ghost mother has a profound impact on your emotional, physical, and spiritual well-being. It can be difficult to understand the connections between being raised by a ghost mother, and the problems you are currently experiencing. It can be equally difficult to understand why something that happened years ago continues to haunt you in the present. This chapter explores the effects of growing up as a ghost-daughter, with the goal of identifying why it hurts so much to be raised this way, and using this information to design a comprehensive plan for healing.

Some women find that focusing on the details of what they didn't get as a child brings up painful memories, but the purpose of doing so isn't to discourage you. On the contrary, we're doing this to validate all that you've experienced, and to increase your understanding of the substantial impact this has had on you. Clarifying the messages that you've carried since childhood is essential in understanding what haunts you, and in shining light on the key aspects that hold you back from getting what you want as an adult.

You've experienced considerable pain in being raised by a ghost mother, and as a result you've missed out on the nurturing, guidance, and support that someone with a real mother takes for granted. While this has contributed to your suffering, I want to encourage you to begin to adopt a perspective that the benefit of your pain is this: you've learned critical skills, and tapped into crucial strengths that can now be used to heal from the past. While there may be times when you envy someone who grew up with a mother who adored and nurtured her, that daughter did not learn, and does know what you do. At this point you don't know all that you've learned from your ghost mother because it's buried under tons of debris, labeled pain and suffering, but as we continue moving forward there will be an increased emphasis on the positive aspects of what you've gained from this experience.

Now, let's answer some of the questions you may have related to growing up with a ghost mother to include: *Why does this hurt so much? Why am I still haunted by this pain when it happened long ago? Why does having a ghost mother mean that I'm still suffering on a daily basis? Am I ever going to get over this pain?* Let's answer these questions by exploring the impact of growing up with a mother who wasn't really there. In doing so, we'll explore what you didn't get due to being inadequately mothered, and the long-term effects that have haunted you into adulthood. It's important to understand this pain in order to overcome it. When you better understand how being mothered by a ghost has affected you, this will help empower you to become the person you want to be.

Let's look at the primary issues that contribute to being haunted by a ghost mother. As you read through this list, pay attention to the descriptions that fit your situation, the ones that resonate strongly for you:

- **There continues to be a strong longing within you for the mother you never had.** This rings true for almost every ghost daughter I've known; it's certainly been true for me. This longing to bond with, and get what we need, from the most significant caretaker in our life is a primitive, and very basic need that when not satisfied leaves a deep sense of lack, emptiness and loss.

- **It's difficult to learn how to develop a sense of identity from someone who doesn't have this for herself.** Ideally, a mother helps her child develop a strong sense of identity during the formative years. When growing up it's essential to have her reflect back what she sees in you, in order for you to figure out who you are. For women, our same sexed parent is the role model who provides this critical information to us. But a mother who is illusive, and hasn't developed a sense of identity, is ill equipped to guide us in this regard.

- **Having heard negative, critical, or demeaning messages from your ghost mother, you've now internalized them, and no longer question their validity.** Not all ghost mothers rage, control, or demean their daughters, but the ones who do leave a strong impression. Long after we leave home, or our mother dies, these negative messages continue to be repeated in our brains. Our mother may no longer say negative things to us, but we continue to say them to ourselves, often without even recognizing that we're doing so.

- **You were taught how to live and be in the world, by someone who doesn't know how to do this herself.** A ghost mother is an illusive presence, a woman compensating for her own feelings of inadequacy with behaviors that make her emotionally unavailable. She can't teach us what she doesn't know, so she often passes her pain on to us, and is unable to teach us coping strategies, or other necessary tools to deal with the challenges life presents.

- **Instead of being well mothered you grew up having to provide attention, nurturing, or support to your mother.** In the process of trying to get what you needed from your mother, unhealthy patterns may permeate your relationship to include doing things for her she could do for herself, feeling responsible for her happiness, or enabling her addiction. In this scenario roles are reversed which creates resentment and anger, and means that you learn how to care for others, but you don't learn how to take care of yourself.

Growing up with a ghost mother haunts us because it hurts so much, and because we miss out on many important aspects of growing up. At the core of the painful feelings that linger into adulthood is usually this question: *If my own mother doesn't love me, then who will?* This is a question that resonates with daughters raised by a mother who was not there in important ways; it festers in our minds, and makes us feel unloved, and inadequate. There's a considerable amount of shame for daughters in this regard, a deep sense that there is something fundamentally wrong with us because we're unable to get what we needed in this crucial relationship. We compare ourselves to others who are able to do so, and wonder why we can't.

Perhaps if we asked, most ghost mothers would say that they love their children, and maybe they do, but when this isn't expressed emotionally, or behaviorally, the result is a child who feels unloved, and unwanted. A mother who doesn't demonstrate acceptance, admiration, love, or attention isn't perceived as a nurturing mother, and isn't meeting the needs of the child she brought into the world. In the introduction to her book **Difficult Mothers**, Terri Apter captures the essence of this pain when she describes that the negative message taken from this experience is: "They persist in seeing themselves as the child who could not secure comfort with the most important person in their life." This statement captures the essence of the pain I've experienced growing up with a ghost mother. I wonder if it does for you?

A ghost mother is a phantom presence in our lives; she isn't someone we can rely on, put our trust in, respect, or share our dreams with. She's unable to give us what we need to navigate our childhood, and emerge from adolescence with confidence, and an intact sense of self. A ghost mother doesn't provide a sense of security, and doesn't impart that we are talented or unique. We spend years denying that she's an illusion, and then are forced to grieve the reality that she is. We need her to be real but she isn't, we need her to guide us, but she can't. We want so badly for her to be real, able to show us how to live, and feel good about ourselves.

As a result of being raised by a ghost mother there is a common constellation of issues that most daughters' struggle with to include:

- **A deep sense of emptiness.**
- **Confusion about our identity.**
- **Insecurity and lack of confidence.**
- **Ignoring our needs to put others first.**
- **Fear of abandonment.**
- **Raw emotions that are easily triggered.**
- **Numbing of emotions.**
- **A sense of shame.**
- **Distorted views of love and relationships.**
- **High tolerance for other's inappropriate behavior.**
- **A focus on lack, i.e. what we don't have.**
- **A profound sense of unworthiness.**

The truth of being raised by a ghost mother is this: your mother wasn't there to take care of you emotionally, wasn't there to nurture or love you when you needed her to do so. She wasn't able to reflect back your beauty or accomplishments, and couldn't offer much-needed guidance, or unconditional love. Without a real mother you have been adrift for most of your life, feeling the absence of a mother to love, guide, and direct you. You needed so much from her, and got so little. For many of us, our ghost mother took considerably more than she ever gave. Maternal neglect during the formative years of our lives impacts each of us differently, depending on many factors to include: your personality, coping style, the availability of other nurturing adults, and the core cause of your mother's illusiveness. My method of coping was to assume the role of the dutiful daughter, completely willing to disregard my own needs in order to be loved, and accepted by my mother.

Here's how other daughters describe the impact of being raised by a ghost mother.

Michelle reacted by focusing on her physical appearance.

My Mom was so controlling that I began not eating, and turned into an anorexic teenager. Even when I had hunger pangs, I would deny myself food. I think subconsciously it was the one thing in life that I had some control over; how much I ate. All my life, I've thought something was wrong with me. I was anxious around others, and never felt good enough, but I couldn't pinpoint why I felt this way. In high school people would tell me that I was very attractive, and I was even asked if I had thought about modeling. But no matter what anyone in the outside world said, deep inside I felt ugly and small.

Lynne has struggled with being able to express herself and develop meaningful connections with others.

I grew up with lack of trust and self-esteem. I became an addict in my efforts to numb my emotional pain. I feel lonely and empty, like I don't belong anywhere. I have no genuine connections due to my inability to create common ground with people, personal disclosure is difficult for me; it's hard to find the middle ground. Sharing too much makes people feel uncomfortable, sharing too little makes me seem standoffish. As I grew older, I became embarrassed, and fearful that someone would think I was similar to my mother in any way, or that if they met her, it would possibly tarnish their perception of me.

Tanya describes numerous health problems as the result of growing up with a ghost mother.

Physical symptoms have been part of my life since I was a teenager. I had an incidence of tetany (muscle spasms), which I now understand occurred because I was so angry with both of my parents. I had recurrent bladder infections for years, also endometriosis. I was hospitalized briefly for depression when I was 19 years old. Several years ago I was diagnosed with cancer, and I firmly believe that stress from my upbringing, and staying in a stressful job situation, were certainly contributing factors.

I am always expecting anger and criticism from others. When I do feel unfairly criticized, or think that I am, I can lose it in huge, overreacting incidents of anger. I've developed considerable anger because of both my parent's treatment of me, and my mother's failure in protecting me from my father's sexual abuse. I know that when I was younger I was acting out a lot of my pain and anger.

Jody has internalized fears from her mother's threats of suicide, and frequent negative messages to her.

I feel empty, and experience serious anxiety when I'm around my mom. Today I still worry that if someone is upset, they may commit suicide, just because of me being alive. It feels like I'm unwanted, and it's often a burden to know how to live in the world. Because of what I've been through, I have intense radar for how others feel, so that I can try to do what they want in order to feel safe. Because of how my mother treated me, I never have felt okay to just be me. I've always felt that I needed to change into someone very different so that I could finally get her acceptance and love. I feel like I was really raised by Snow White's evil stepmother.

Susan describes her constant striving to be doing things, and what drives her to act this way.

I am a master at reading others, and a failure at reading myself. My emotional needs were always secondary to my mother's perceived needs, and in many other relationships I have subjugated my needs to those of others. I am driven by a little machine inside me to make everyone else happy. I am in constant motion; I can't sit still for any length of time because there is an internal drive that powers me to always do more.

One thing I've noticed recently is that I'm averse to making long-term commitments. I believe the reason is that my mother has sucked the life out of me so now I fear that if I get involved with something that's demanding, I may feel smothered in much the same ways. I am not at peace with myself, and usually feel some element of anxiety. I am never satisfied with anything I do, and I attribute this to the way that I was raised, with no sense of affirmation, or value. This has left a huge hole in my heart that I try so hard to fill. I know intellectually that I can't fill it by always being active, and productive, a "doer", but what I know intellectually, and what drives me emotionally are different.

Why You Are Haunted by the Pain of Your Past

It is not until you become a mother that your judgment slowly turns to compassion and understanding. This quote by Erma Bombeck, a woman best known for offering humorous insights, (I guess from our perspective it *is* humorous!) captures the usual expectations for a mother's role; someone who learns to recognize and put her child's needs first. It got me thinking about the norms in our society, the expectations of mother as a source of comfort. Growing up *not* receiving this type of care makes it very difficult for those with mothers who didn't treat us in compassionate ways. In receiving minimal attention and concern from her, we also have to come to terms with a maternal experience that's vastly different from the majority of the population. It often can be difficult to get empathy from friends or relatives, to share openly about what it was like growing up, or to describe the issues that continue to haunt us. Often, we are not believed or are accused of exaggerating the difficulties of our experience.

Recently I had the opportunity to attend a presentation by the Dalai Lama. I was surprised when His Holiness began by talking about the importance of receiving affection as a child, in order to develop a sense of security and a good self-image. He cited the example of baby turtles; born with mothers who don't watch over them, and described this situation as "very unfortunate." "Compassion for all," he explained, "begins with affection when we are young." This is a truth he considers so important that he shared a story about his mother, fondly remembering when he sat on her shoulders, and used her ears to direct where he wanted to go! I felt so validated in my mother-related struggles while listening to this deeply spiritual man focus on how this critical maternal relationship is so essential to each of us as individuals, and in creating a world that embraces peace.

In growing up inadequately mothered, there are other external factors that further confuse our perspective about being raised by a ghost to include:

- **The taboo in our society in regards to speaking unkindly about one's mother.** It's difficult to share the truth about a ghost mother when responses include: *But she's your mother. Everyone blames their mother for their problems. Maybe you're being too hard on her. She doesn't seem that bad to me.* These responses further compound our pain by minimizing our difficulties in dealing with a ghost mother, and discourage us from discussing the truth of our experience.

- **Living in a society that rarely acknowledges a mother who doesn't meet the ideal of being nurturing, and loving.** This reality leaves ghost-daughters feeling isolated during holidays such as Mother's Day, as we don't have loving stories to share, or nurturing memories of mom to bring us comfort. Hallmark doesn't sell cards that speak to our experience. There are plenty of holidays in which happy families are pictured having fun together, and when this isn't how things were for you, it's particularly difficult to be reminded that your efforts to emotionally connect with, and be loved by your mother, were never reciprocated.

- **Family members who disagree with your perception of your ghost mother's emotional unavailability.** Several factors can contribute to this dynamic. The first-born child often has a different experience with a ghost mother than do children who arrive later. An older child may provide attention and care to younger children so they don't have as strong a sense of not being nurtured. If the first child caters to the mother's needs, then less may be expected of her siblings in this regard. A child born after several other siblings may be more neglected by a ghost mother who is already feeling overwhelmed. Females are likely to have more problems with a ghost mother than male siblings, because mom is her primary same-sexed role model.

- **Mental health professionals who don't understand your experience can make you feel even worse.** There are currently a limited number of mental health professionals who truly understand the dynamics of growing up with a ghost mother. This is partly due to the fact that these issues have been shrouded in secrecy for so many years. Women have been reluctant to reveal the truth of their experience, and often are not believed. Dr. McBride's book, which is still the only book addressing issues specific to daughters' of narcissistic mothers, was not published until 2008. Information on this topic has simply not been available until very recently, and is still quite limited. As a result, mental health professionals have not known what to look for, what to ask, or how to help when these issues are revealed. As more ghost-daughters share what this experience is really like, and its devastating impact, I believe more will be done by the mental health profession to understand this illusive problem, in order to better respond with compassionate and effective healing strategies.

Susan tells a poignant story of seeking help from a therapist for issues with her ghost mother, and receiving terrible advice.

I tried joint therapy with my mother, I was still seeking her validation, love, and affirmation, and I thought we could talk through our issues. I was soon to retire from a successful career; I knew that she was salivating over the concept of my retirement, as she wanted me to be her caretaker. I did not want that onerous obligation so I went to a local therapist to give me the strength to set boundaries with my mother. The counselor inquired, "What is your goal for counseling?" I responded that my goal was to be affirmed by my mother, and to hear her say that she loved me. My mother said that the only problem was that I go on trips with my husband, and don't take her.

The conversation then got stuck on this one point, that I was responsible for the "most pain she had ever experienced in her life," by "abandoning" her to occasionally vacation with my husband. The therapist obviously felt sorry for my mother, who is a master at portraying herself as a victim, and felt she had to fix the problem of the negligent daughter. She looked up cruises that departed from this area, downloaded the information, handed it to me, and told me to take my mother on a cruise so she "wouldn't feel so hurt and excluded."

This was the absolute last thing I wanted to do, take a cruise with my mother and spend the entire time as her "lackey." I went to therapy to get away from her intrusive personality, not to be told to be responsible for her. A worse situation with my mother was created as the result of a therapist who absolutely did NOT understand, and who was sucked into feeling sorry for my "poor, pathetic mother." Perhaps she should go on a cruise with my mother—I'm not!

A pattern develops in which efforts to connect with your mother are not achieved, and this pain is further reinforced by external responses that don't support the reality of being raised by a ghost mother. When viewed from this perspective it becomes easier to see why many years later, we still continue to be haunted on so many different levels. Some of what we learn from this experience becomes adaptive, but to a greater extent it is frustrating, and confusing. Efforts to cope with this pain can become self-destructive, such as numbing feelings with drugs or alcohol, or looking for love in relationships that echo these familiar, abusive patterns. As a result of growing up ghost mothered we ultimately don't feel loved, grounded or guided.

The Many Ways Pain Manifests When It's Not Dealt With

With so many painful feelings to deal with, so much confusion, and so little support, it's no wonder we attempt to deny this painful reality. Growing up this way encourages us to pretend that we're happy when we're not, to do things we don't want to do, to blame ourselves for problems in our relationships.

The dynamics that exist in a ghost family are similar to other dysfunctional families in which feelings are ignored, and awful incidents denied. Feeling uncomfortable in this painful reality, struggling to feel better, a child who openly questions the lack of nurturing is often blamed or ignored, rather than comforted, as it's difficult for other family members to cope with this reality as well. This type of response can also occur when attempting to discuss this issue with other family members, as an adult. I mention this because it's common for a ghost daughter to want to try to help her mother, and in making this effort she may want to engage the help of others in the family. This rarely goes well, and it's important to keep in mind that it's not your responsibility to try to fix the cause of your mother's illusiveness. Your efforts to do so are likely to be rebuffed by all involved. Dr. Christiane Northrup, an empowering advocate for women's health, offered this advice on a PBS special: *Your mother has a higher power, and it isn't you!*

The reality that we grow up *not* getting what we need takes its toll on us, and significantly impacts us at every level of our functioning. We spend years trying to get what we need from our ghost mother, and as a result our entire being is negatively affected. This is why the problems that keep coming up in your life, to include health issues, depression, difficulty in relationships, a sense of emptiness, feeling stuck, and many others, are indicators of pain that goes much deeper. When the true source of your pain isn't dealt with, it will show up in various ways until it is acknowledged, and addressed. My lingering ghost issues came to light primarily through continued health problems, which was annoying and frustrating, and made me feel that I had little control over my own body, much less my life. When I came to understand that this pattern would continue until I faced the root causes, I became very motivated to work through, and come to terms with the pain that I'd internalized.

I grew up not liking myself very much, doubting my own perceptions, and living with a deep sense that I didn't deserve to be happy. In my efforts to cope, I developed an outward presentation as someone who was functioning pretty well, most of the time I even believed this pretense. In reality, I was fearful of many things, and was filled with negative thoughts about myself, and my ability to get my needs met. I felt sad and insecure, but worked hard to keep these feelings to myself. Pretending to be okay is what I learned growing up, and I incorporated this instruction into my efforts to manage my life. *Fake it, look good on the outside*, is what I was taught, but in the long term it simply wasn't working, my inner self wasn't fooled by this charade.

The problems that developed for me as the result of being raised by a ghost mother demonstrate that the issues haunting us exist because they are a reflection of the core issues that we haven't yet resolved. There is an intriguing feedback system in humans, as we are perfectly equipped to heal, if we listen and pay attention to what our minds and bodies are trying to tell us. Whether it's a behavior pattern that keeps repeating, a health problem that continues to occur, or a general dissatisfaction with the way we feel, we are designed to prosper when we embrace these problems, and look for the source of what is causing them. When you learn that you've been deeply impacted by a ghost mother, you are given the opportunity to address these important issues by embracing this wisdom, rather than ignoring it, or dealing only with the symptom itself.

Michelle describes the connections she's made between issues she struggles with, and being raised by an illusive mother who taught her to dislike herself.

Physically, I have had various neurological issues, and even some unexplained tachycardia, in which I become tired much easier than normal. This was much more noticeable in my teen years. Emotionally, I have had a serious battle with anxiety, and intermittent, serious depressive episodes. I've even tried to harm myself three times, mostly because I've internalized the message from my ghost mother that I was bad, and that there was something evil about me, even though I've always been gentle and kind with others.

Being raised by a ghost mother becomes a traumatic experience over time, and these difficulties often manifest in the body. I asked Dr. Carolle Jean-Murat to further explain, based on her personal and professional experience, some of the ways that being raised by a ghost mother creates health problems, and specific indicators that this is what's happening in our bodies. She has generously shared information related to this topic that was written for her upcoming book, **Is It Your Hormones, Or Something Else?**

I've worked with women who were feeling increasingly depressed, had difficulty sleeping, experienced decreased appetite, fatigue, diminished libido, and were easily overwhelmed. They had no idea that their physical and emotional symptoms were related to their family situation.

During the first four years of life—and I believe that it starts in the womb—a child needs someone who offers comfort, love, acceptance, and security. If these needs are not met, it will affect how that child feels about herself, and how she relates to the world. From ages 4-8, the development of self-esteem also depends on what happens at school, with friends, in the neighborhood, and on television. However, parents are the most influential in the development of your self-esteem, and how you perceive and value yourself. To have healthy self-esteem, a child has to feel loved unconditionally not for what she does, but for who she is.

It is not uncommon that unresolved issues with a parent, or caregiver, will resurface during a woman's life when they are sick. The appearance of symptoms can be likened to the body's intuitive wisdom, reminding the person that these old wounds have to be resolved. To me, we are like a coil, in which "being perfect," would be a straight wire. With time, when we realize that's who we are, the coil is an impediment to our emotional and physical well-being. We do our best to change the coil into that straight wire, and with all our strength we hold it in both hands and try to stretch it out. While everything is going fine, there is no problem keeping that wire straight, but as soon as we are under stress, we spring back to being that coiled wire. Many women are surprised that their present situation is deeply rooted to their past. It is simply your inner wisdom, signaling you over and over, that it is time to heal these past issues!

Growing up mothered poorly by a ghost often leaves us spiritually bereft, feeling alone, unloved, victimized, afraid to trust, and struggling with the concept of forgiveness.

Jody shares her thoughts about how this experience makes believing in a higher power extremely difficult.

I've developed a lack of faith for a being greater than myself. Trusting or believing in an authority figure, or a creator, is impossible for me as my birth Mom was an un-trustworthy and dangerous person to be around.

Tanya discusses the ongoing development of her spiritual path.

I was turned off to any type of spiritual or religious exploration because my mother was extremely religious, and pious, which turned me off. Initially, I tried my best to forge my own spiritual path within a conventional religious practice. I was strongly influenced by existentialism, and Native-American teachings, but I struggled to develop a relationship with God. How could I believe in a higher power when I'd been treated so poorly by my own parents? In the past year I've found a new spiritual home with the Unitarian Universalist Church, I like the emphasis on personal spiritual search, and the acceptance of all spiritual beliefs as worthy.

In using the term *spiritual*, I mean exploring the existence of a higher power, in addition to developing a better understanding of the inherent wisdom inside us, which is our spirit. I've come to believe this is a critical aspect of healing from a ghost mother, to honestly face what we've been through, how we've responded, and to successfully integrate this painful experience into our sense of self. The perspective that we embrace in coming to terms with our experience is essential to moving forward, and viewing ourselves in a positive light. I've learned it's extremely helpful to focus on these essential aspects of who we are in order to deepen our understanding, and learn from the commonality of the human experience.

Often, we don't get the chance to explore the intuitive, inner aspects of our experience as we're growing up, but we do get the opportunity as we begin to heal. Previously we were so focused on getting our basic needs met that caring for ourselves, or asking questions about the deeper meaning of life seemed like a luxury we couldn't afford. I didn't consider spiritual ideas to be an important part of my healing journey until I had made considerable progress in coming to terms with my pain, and came to understand the importance of nurturing my spirit. I now see that these concepts go hand in hand with emotional healing. This simple quote by the Dalai Lama captures how spirituality can enhance the process of healing: *Pain is inevitable. Suffering is optional.*

The following journal entry that I wrote prior to discovering spiritual ideas show how frustrated and angry I was, and how much I stood to gain from better understanding the concepts of forgiveness, letting go, and believing in a higher power.

I still hang on to anger about being treated so badly by her. Not only her inability to see me, or nurture me as my mother, but to then continue into my adulthood as an angry, mean, critical presence in my life—that's been really tough, and clearly I'm not over it. I also hold onto a great deal of shame about this situation. I'm embarrassed that my mother acts the way she does, and that I have been unable to have a positive relationship with her. And although I know it was killing me to stay involved with her, I still carry a sense of guilt that somehow I should have figured out a way to do so.

When I wrote this I was at a point where I couldn't forgive myself, and I couldn't forgive my mother. Opening myself to the possibility of viewing my pain differently allowed me to embrace new and comforting concepts that were very helpful. Spiritual awareness can be very effective in finding answers to questions such as: *Why me? How do I deal with my suffering? How can I forgive someone who has hurt me so much? How do I move forward from where I am now?*

The spiritual pain that we experience in growing up with a ghost mother is often overlooked, yet these concepts are soothing, informative, and can change the very essence of how we come to terms with our pain. You will learn more about exploring and implementing spiritual solutions to the pain of a ghost mother in the upcoming chapters. Growing up with the pain of an illusive mother is haunting for many reasons, and affects you in ways you may not have recognized until now. Start to consider how your pain is being expressed through your body, mind, and spirit because we are on a journey to identify, and heal the many ways that you've been impacted by this experience.

In ending this chapter I want to share a vivid dream that I had several days after attending Dr. McBride's workshop, in which daughters of narcissistic mothers were united in healing. This dream had a powerful impact on me; when I woke up I could still picture all the details in my mind. My interpretation is that it represents how much I learned at this conference, how much my mind and spirit were "colored" by this experience, and how profoundly I was inspired. In the final analysis I think this dream is about how much hope there is in healing, and how much there is to be gained in taking the journey to do so.

My Ice Cave Dream

I enter an ice cave with a few other people, there is a leader who encourages and supports us. The opening is small and I feel very anxious, as I hate small spaces and the sense of being trapped or confined, and unable to control my destiny.

The cave is covered in ice, there's ice on the ground and large icicles hanging from the top. We are encouraged to keep going, at the same time that our fears are acknowledged, and we are told that what we'll see at the end is well worth the journey. On our feet we have spiky shoes that make it possible to walk on ice. In our hands we have spikes to jam into the ice when needed.

We go along for a while; I have to keep encouraging myself to stay on this journey. We come to a place where a wooden ladder goes down into a larger room, and climb down it, one person at a time. This room is much larger and I immediately feel better, we walk in this room for a while, and then enter an even larger area where a small stream is moving along the left side.

This startles me and I ask how there can be a stream flowing when everything else is frozen? The answer, it's a natural underground hot spring. The water is so hot that it doesn't freeze and in fact, as we venture further steam and mist are rising from it that fills the room.

The person leading us now suggests we sit in a certain area and wait. "Wait for what?" we ask. "Just wait," he replies, "it will happen soon and it will be well worth the wait."

And so we wait. Soon we see rays of light coming through cracks in the cave walls. The light comes through and mingles with the moisture of the hot spring, and the cold ice—the result is hundreds of rainbows filling the room, pieces of colored light are dancing everywhere. And yes, this sight is more than worth the journey, and the time spent waiting for it to happen.

Exercise for this chapter:

This is an easy one. The purpose is to introduce how scents and smells can influence and shift your mood. For example, the wonderful aroma of baking cookies can provide comfort, bring back happy memories, or make you want to pour a cold glass of milk to enjoy the cookies the minute they come out of the oven.

You can use the basic concepts of **aromatherapy** in a variety of positive, healing ways. The smell of lavender oil is very soothing, if you like the smell just dab some of this essential oil (available at health food stores) on your arm, or add to a bath. Jasmine oil is stimulating for most people, and can be used to improve energy. Some people resonate with smells more than others. Have fun with this exercise, to include lighting candles that are scented in a way that appeals to you.

CHAPTER 5

NO MORE GHOST STORIES

**Coming to terms with the mother
who wasn't.**

You must do the thing you think you cannot do.
~ Eleanor Roosevelt

Your Mother Can't Give What She Doesn't Have

The process of healing starts with a shift in thinking, a
shift that dramatically changes your perception of the
past, and your relationship with your ghost mother. This
transformation begins when you recognize, and begin to
work with the truth of this statement: *Your ghost mother is
doing the best she can.*

I realize this may not initially appear to make sense, and
that it may seem to minimize the pain you've been through,
as well as the longing for a nurturing mother that continues

to haunt you. Keep in mind that your mother is a ghost for good reason, whether her emotional disconnection is due to mental illness, addiction, the lousy childhood she experienced, or other factors that have negatively impacted her emotional development. The result is that when you deal with a ghost mother, what you get from her is all she has to give.

It's common when raised this way to mistakenly believe that you are the one with the problem, and that your mother is reacting to something you did, or didn't do. I held on to this illusion for many years, convinced I needed to think, feel or behave differently, taking the blame for my mother's inability to love me. I held on to the hope that she was going to become a better mother; that she would somehow develop nurturing qualities. I couldn't "let go of the rope" that kept us connected, refused to believe that this was all she had to offer—not when I still needed so much from her. But holding on to this perception just doesn't jive with reality. If your mother did have nurturing maternal qualities, it's a pretty sure bet she wouldn't be hiding them from you. Being a mother is a tough job, being a nurturing one is even more of a challenge. Not all women are cut out for this job, particularly if she wasn't well-mothered, or is impacted by mental or physical illness. The way she interacts with you is her best version of mothering—no matter how inadequate, or hurtful it feels to you.

What you are reacting to, what is causing you so much pain, are the emotional deficits within her, the inability to connect with or care about you because responding to her own needs is a full-time job. Your ghost mother, with all her inadequacies, is putting forth her best effort, doing the best she can. While her performance may rate no higher than an "F," even on her best days, the point is that she can't provide good mothering when the capacity to do so doesn't exist inside of her. She can't nurture you when she doesn't experience the emotions that elicit this response. She can't guide you in life when she's blindly making her way through it. She can't love you when she doesn't love herself.

Yes, there are a few exceptions to this bleak scenario. A mildly impaired ghost mother might consider getting help if she's suffering from an addiction or depression. The improved insight, and coping skills she develops *could* improve her ability to better tune into you emotionally. Some ghost mothers do become aware of personal or parenting issues and are able to make positive changes by utilizing therapy, or other avenues for self-improvement. The length of time you've been dealing with your ghost mother, the intensity of her illusiveness, and her ability to communicate are all indicators of her ability to make changes. For example, an alcoholic mother might get a DUI, and be court ordered into counseling. A narcissistic mother is unlikely to seek help, but she could become depressed (as previously mentioned by Dr. Patton) at the loss of a relationship, and decide to seek help in this regard.

Realistically, I would not suggest waiting around for this to happen, and it's important to be clear, this happens only when a ghost mother is motivated to deal with her issues or to grow emotionally, and has the capacity to do so. New and improved ghost mothers are the exception. Most of us are stuck with the one who is not expected to improve, and who may continue to get worse as she ages. In most cases, she's incapable of self-reflection or making changes, and she's not going to become a different person because you need her to. She struggles with issues that you may, or may not be aware of, and is currently putting her best foot forward. In other words, she's giving *all* she has to give in her role as your mother. And while her efforts fall far short of providing the mothering you need and deserve, what you've gotten from her so far is likely all that you can expect to receive.

It's critically important to understand that this type of mother isn't deliberately providing lousy mothering; the issues that contribute to her illusive nature are the same ones that make her emotionally unavailable. She doesn't consciously choose to fall short of being a fully functioning mother, and if there was a way for her to look objectively at what she's not able to provide, I'd like to think she'd be upset with her poor performance. But, this isn't a decision that's under her control; being a ghost is her destiny, for whatever reason. When you are able to shift your perspective to accept that this is how things are, rather than avoiding this reality, you'll view your mother in a dramatically different way, and this changes everything because it allows you to heal, and to move forward. When you come to see that it's her illusive behavior that defines her, you will no longer hold on to unrealistic expectations for what she can provide.

The primary reason there is so much distress associated with being raised by a ghost mother is the emotional pain that's created by the unmet longing for a real mother. This pain manifests itself throughout our being, impacting all aspects of who we are. When you start to incorporate the reality of your mother's limitations, you create a new (and more accurate) perspective, one in which you have choices you previously didn't know existed.

Most of us don't realize how much damage chasing our ghost mother can create within us; focusing considerable energy on our longing to be nurtured is exhausting, and makes it difficult for us to grow up. I think because we've always done this, we don't question this unhealthy way of interacting with her, it becomes the norm; the way things are. Untangling yourself from the bind of longing for, and chasing a ghost mother, requires making peace with her illusiveness. Not doing so means continuing to chase her misty presence, desperately hoping to receive what she doesn't have to give. Your ability to heal requires defining her role in your life differently than you have up to this point, it requires making a decision to emotionally let go of the ghost that is never going to turn into a real mother.

As you develop a more realistic perspective of what your ghost mother does, and doesn't have to offer, intense emotions, and other reactions, will gradually dissipate. This isn't to say that you won't continue to feel a deep desire for nurturing from her, but the intensity will decrease when you accept this reality, and as you learn new ways to get your needs met. Re-defining your maternal relationship is very powerful because it releases both you, and your mother, from unrealistic expectations. An additional benefit to viewing your mother's role in your life in a different way is that it shifts the power in your relationship. You will no longer be willing to put up with whatever she dishes out, in the misguided hope that doing so will result in the payoff you're looking for. The result of making this shift is the knowledge that as long as you hold onto your longing for a real mother, you can't heal from the pain of not having one.

Compassion for What Haunts Her

Having to come to terms with the fact that your ghost mother isn't who you need her to be is challenging, as is letting go of the long-term desire to get more from her. At the same time, the ability to do so contains the ultimate source of your healing, and will provide you with peace, power and freedom. When you come to see this situation for what it is, there is a sense of relief, an acknowledgement of what your inner wisdom has perhaps always known. When you reach out to touch a ghost, your hand goes right through. This is all there is to her, so how can this illusive presence possibly provide the nurturing you need?

Your ally in letting go of the relationship with your ghost mother is the concept of compassion, for yourself and for your mother. Applying this concept contributes further to making a positive shift in your perspective. By definition, compassion means to have an awareness of what another person is feeling, along with a desire to alleviate their suffering. Having compassion for yourself means recognizing that what you want from your mother is reasonable, and that your maternal desires are normal. It's not the longing to be nurtured that's problematic; it's your ghost mother's inability to meet those needs. As long as you continue to chase the vision of a loving mother, you are going to come up empty handed. It's time to give yourself a break, to recognize your longing for what it is, a deeply ingrained desire we are born with, to be taken care of, and loved. The longing isn't the problem, you are not the problem—the problem is that your mother doesn't have the capacity to satisfy this longing.

At the same time, developing some compassion for your mother is also important, facing the truth that she isn't fully present, and that it isn't her choice to be this way. It's helpful to increase your awareness that she's an emotionally wounded woman struggling to understand herself, and her own life, and that this is why she's incapable of positively impacting yours. When you stop chasing her, stop making demands and holding onto unrealistic expectations, not only does this release you from the struggle, it releases her as well.

Use compassionate thoughts, feelings, and actions to loosen your grip on the struggle for love that you're engaged in with your mother. Healing truly starts when you let go of her emotionally, in a loving manner, when you allow yourself to accept there's no way she can provide what you need. When you find ways to do so, the struggle that is keeping you stuck comes to an end. When you stop chasing this illusive ghost, you will start to heal in profound ways. The energy in you, and in your relationship with her, will shift so that you can recognize, and deal with the situation as it really is.

You can't change the past. You can't change your mother. The only thing you do have control over is how you view who your ghost mother really is. Coming to terms with her limitations, and your inability to change this reality, creates healing in ways that no other solution can. Stop looking for maternal love where it doesn't exist. Take charge of yourself. Start creating your own life; seek nurturing in ways that are likely to succeed. This song, originally recorded by Bonnie Raitt, started playing as I was writing this chapter; the lyrics perfectly describe the dilemma of having a ghost mother:

> *I can't make you love me if you don't.*
> *You can't make your heart feel something*
> *that it won't.*

In a conventional ghost story, the threat is usually external, running away from a ghost that is chasing you. In this story, the threat is an internal one, based on how you decide to let this experience impact you, and what you tell yourself about it. Healing requires a profound shift in your way of thinking, and being in the world. Utilize the ghost-busting strategies presented later in this book so that you stop focusing on what you don't have—on the sense of lack that inevitably comes from being raised by a ghost mother, to focusing on the areas where you *do* have power, where you can get what you want, and absolutely deserve.

Stop Longing and Start Living

The nurturing you seek does not exist within your mother; it exists within you. What you didn't get from your ghost mother has helped shape you into the person you are today, and now you have the opportunity to build on what you've learned in ways that serve you. The love you've sought from her can be found elsewhere. In order to find sources for your unmet maternal needs, it's helpful to identify the *coping style* you've used to deal with your mother. Doing so provides information about your personality, coping skills, and intuitive choices that will help you in making important decisions about healing. Keep in mind that we don't consciously choose our particular coping style; it's a function of many factors.

There are three distinct styles used to cope with a ghost mother:

- **PLACATING your mother.** This response attempts to please and appease her. This coping style is about soothing the ghost mother, trying to make her happy, responding to her needs. This style attempts to deal directly with the problem by doing what is expected, believing this will help you to feel better, and improve the situation. The downside of this style is the constant need to repress your desires, which is particularly painful if the placating efforts do not pay off.

- **REBELLING against your mother.** This response
  is in many ways the opposite of the placating style.
  In this style the focus is to oppose her, either in an
  effort to show that you don't need her, or based on the
  belief that it's not worth the effort to keep trying. This
  is a more indirect style, an effort to avoid repeating
  behaviors that don't get results. The rebel gives up
  trying to get her needs met, and may be indirectly
  attempting to get the ghost mother to respond to her.
  The downside of this style is that it can turn into efforts
  to get revenge, or to "show" the mother what a lousy
  job she's doing, in ways that are self-destructive.

- **IGNORING your mother.** This response is a variation
  on the rebelling style, one that is also emotionally
  avoidant, but with the absence of associated "acting
  out" behaviors. This is a style in which you try to deal
  with your mother as infrequently as possible, expecting
  little from her, and staying out of her way as much as
  possible. This style is one that may develop over time,
  as a reaction to not getting positive responses from
  her.

These styles aren't superior or inferior to the other; they
are different ways of coping with an extremely difficult
situation, variations on the extent to which you responded
by being either engaged or disengaged from your ghost
mother. There can also be a mixture of coping styles, for
example someone with a rebellious style still might hide in

the closet in order to avoid her mother. Each of these styles has adaptive and maladaptive aspects. Placating may help in avoiding angry arguments, but at the same time constantly feeling like a failure in dealing with your mother can take a toll on your psyche. Awareness of your coping style when dealing with stress, or situations in which you feel powerless, is useful in creating different ways of responding, and taking care of yourself.

My coping style was trying to placate my mother, doing my best to go along with her demands, in the hope of keeping the peace, and getting what I needed from her. When this wasn't effective, I eventually ended up adopting an ignoring style. Here's an example of the rebelling style, as told by **Lynne:** *I would shut her out, disengage, distance myself from hearing her emotionally, and if I could, physically disappear as well.*

There is a limit to how much you can do, a limit to how long you continue to try to obtain your mother's love. When you're convinced that chasing doesn't work, then it's time to change direction. Focusing on your ghost mother as a source of comfort and doggedly seeking this from her gets you nowhere, and creates a repetitive pattern that keeps you stuck. These patterns change only when they are consciously examined, and replaced by strategies that *do* work.

The problems that make your mother a ghost have often been passed down through many generations, creating a legacy of troubled ghosts. Perhaps your mother adapted to conditions such as abuse or abandonment by developing coping strategies that did not enhance her ability to think, feel or react in useful ways. It's common in dysfunctional families that no one wants to admit these patterns exist, and so they become the norm. Our mothers didn't have many of the resources we are fortunate to have today. When we have the courage to question our lack of mothering, when we take action to feel better, we impact not only our own life, but also can make a significant difference in the lives of others. Don't fall into the same patterns of invisibility that may have haunted your family for generations. Accept and make peace with your ghost mother as she really is, then turn your focus to finding out who you really are, what you need, and how to get those needs met. When you let go of the longing to be nurtured by your mother, the longing for the person she can never be, this dissipates the illusion that will never become reality. Finally, you can get on with the business of living your own life.

Have you ever tried to hug a ghost? You end up hugging yourself. The longing for a real mother *will* diminish as your needs are met in other ways. Giving your ghost mother repeated opportunities to be someone she can't be accomplishes nothing, and establishes patterns and interactions that are damaging to you. Ignoring your pain, or acting it out in self destructive ways is not a solution, it simply postpones facing the reality that your ghost mother isn't there for you. Make a conscious decision, now, to let go of the lack, and the longing. It's never too late to get what you need, and to become the person you want to be. You now have the opportunity to do this for yourself, and you are far more tuned into what you need than your mother ever was. It's time to transcend your mother, and her problems. Decide that *you* will be responsible for what happens next by shifting the power in this relationship to where it needs to be, within you.

Now we are going to shift our focus from understanding the impact of growing up with a ghost mother, to exploring healing strategies designed to move you beyond this pain. To help you begin to see the variety of strategies that can be used, as well as how much improvement they can create, here are some real-life examples from the ghost-daughters who have been telling their stories throughout this book.

Michelle describes the shift in thinking that helped her better understand her ghost mother, and the new perspective she now embraces.

Today, when I look back at things I see how broken my mother is, and I understand better that she was very jealous of my having better opportunities in life than she did. I view her problems now through a different lens. I see that her problems are like a disease, but with no treatment to potentially get rid of the disease. Over the years things have become clearer for me. I see how damaging it was to me to think my duty on earth was to please others. Participating in CoDA groups (Co-Dependents Anonymous) has helped me see that this kind of thinking is learned, and needs to be undone.

Now, I am working on myself, on defining who I am. I spent the early part of my life unable to be myself, because my mother refused to let me be my own person. Now, when I look at her as a "sick" woman instead of someone that "chooses" to be mean, I can deal better with my life, and move forward. I cannot change her; I can only change me, and the ways I react to her.

Lynne continues to feel deep sadness about the way she's grown up, but is learning what she can do to feel better about herself.

I've learned that I'm accountable for my actions and mistakes, never blaming anyone for my choices. I hope my children see this in me; I think they do. I've learned that happiness is my responsibility, that it is a choice, and that meaningful social connections are essential to my happiness. Practicing self-care and self-compassion is a continuing, conscious effort that helps. Deep within myself I know I deserve to be happy, and having the courage to change direction to find fulfilling relationships is something I take pride in. It's really helpful to communicate with my "online-gang" of other daughters who suffer this silent abuse.

I'm learning to disengage from people who don't exhibit reciprocity in relationships, in order to make room for those who do. It's sort of like cleaning out my closet of unworn and outdated clothes, in order to make room for newer and more current fashions. I think the strength gained from growing up without any maternal advocacy has provided me with the knowledge to "self-protect" when needed.

Tanya has recognized the connections between her health and the pain of her past, and is integrating ways to manage her anger and better care for herself.

Knowing what is going on is the first step in healing from the situation. At first you're excited that you finally understand what the deal is. What's been hard for me is facing up to the consequences, and the reality. Discovering that I didn't really have a mother, that she'll never give me a break, and never had any real empathy for me is difficult. Getting free from her control seems necessary in order to heal. The challenges in dealing with this are better than being unconscious about the whole thing, and being hurt over and over again. I'll take the hardship of healing any day.

I've beaten cancer for now, and I no longer have the time, energy or patience for unnecessarily stressful people in my life. I am in therapy and try to find healthy ways to deal with anger. I'm more in touch with my feelings, and my needs. Now, I'm more likely to speak up when I think I'm being taken advantage of, which I couldn't do before because of my past. The spiritual feelings I have these days are based on the wonder and glory I feel for the entire universe.

Jody has made it a point to surround herself with more loving energy, and offers advice about what she did to feel differently about love, and life.

The best thing for me was to get completely outside of my family circle, and spend time with "healthy" families. The ones that say, "I love you," respect each other, don't control others, and are genuinely kind. Did you see the movie, "The Matrix"? Leaving Mom, and the rest of my crazy family for a while made me feel like I was entering a new Matrix, getting away from the dysfunction helped me begin to experience healthy love.

Tell yourself, and find evidence in the world that you DO deserve to be respected for who you already are. Find ways to remind yourself that you are a good, loving, compassionate and kind person, as this is what really matters in life. Love and kindness is what life is all about. Feel proud and good about yourself. Talk to yourself positively, and considerately, as you would talk to a good friend.

Susan now views her mother quite differently, and has developed compassion for her. She's also discovered the importance of nurturing friends.

I don't think my mother has any insight into her behavior, nor the capacity for change. I accept that this is who she is, and I no longer yearn for something I will never have. I understand that she will never be able to love me unconditionally, but there are times when I just want a mother to hold and love me, I expect she probably wanted the same thing.

I make sure that I sustain relationships with others who have healthy personalities, and who are vibrant and vital. They breathe life into me. I am incredibly thankful for friends who listen to me, support and love me, and don't judge me, even though they aren't able to fully understand how a mother cannot love her own daughter.

I've discovered that writing helps purge my soul of the demons of conflict with my mother, and so I write as a way for the internal volcano to erupt, and the lava to flow. Doing so has helped me realize that I have been on a therapeutic journey, and I have made progress. I also make sure that I exercise on a regular basis. Taking a brisk walk clears my head, and when the weather is nice, I ride my bicycle. It lifts my soul. I am now paying much more attention to my own happiness.

In each of these stories, similar themes emerge. Feelings of being defective, internalizing negative messages and an illusive sense of self are amongst the challenges faced by ghost daughters. Growing up with a *lack of maternal advocacy*, as Lynne puts it so well, leaves you feeling lost, and very alone. Now that you recognize the pain of growing up with a ghost mother it's time to focus on moving forward, just as the women in these stories are doing.

It's difficult to feel complete when raised by a mother who hasn't developed a real presence in the world—but you *can* create a life in which you are visible. Your life will continue to improve as you implement the ghost-busting strategies in the next chapter. What you are about to be introduced to is a comprehensive description of the strategies and solutions I used in my healing journey, those that I've discovered in my work with clients, and a few that I came up with while writing this book. Here are answers to the burning question: *What can I do to feel better?*

It's my belief that you will become EMPOWERED (confident and inspired) by working through the strategies in the next chapter. They have completely changed my life, and have introduced hope and healing to many others. Now that you understand the factors contributing to your mother's illusive existence, and have explored the impact on your own life, you have all you need to successfully move past this pain. This process is an exciting journey in which you will get to know yourself, move beyond your mother's limitations, and create a reality that makes you visible. You've been haunted for too long by ghost mother issues, now is the time to decrease your suffering, and increase your passion for living. You deserve a real life, and you can have one.

Exercise for this chapter:

Come up with 3 compassionate statements to say to someone you love.

Here are a few suggestions to get you started: *I am always here for you. I am so impressed with what you did today. It warms my heart when I think about you.*

Write your statements in your journal.

Now picture the person you love, and say each of these statements out loud, notice what it feels like to do so. Does your heart feel light? Is there a sense of happiness in extending this kindness to someone else?

Take a deep breath. Hold it for a second, and then let your breath out slowly.

Now choose one of the compassionate statements, and say it out loud, directing it to yourself.

CHAPTER 6

REFUSING TO LIVE YOUR LIFE AS A GHOST

The importance of being visible.

Healing may not be so much about getting better,
as about letting go of everything that isn't you—all
of the expectations, all of the beliefs—and becoming
who you are.

~ Rachel Naomi Remen

Moving Beyond Ghost Mothering

When I was in second grade I won a contest to promote the school book fair by coming up with the slogan: Look. Buy a book. As the winner I was given the opportunity to take home any book at the fair that I wanted. I knew that I wanted a large, hardcover book with beautiful color pictures of horses; I'd already looked through it several times. Instead, I walked away with a small paperback that I didn't want, and never read. Even at this young age I did not feel worthy of receiving a book that I knew was much more expensive, even though it was my reason for entering the contest. I had earned this book, but when the moment came to claim my prize, I didn't feel entitled to receive what I'd won by coming up with the best slogan.

This example foreshadowed the significant problems that I was going to experience as an adult. As the result of not being nurtured, and constantly being criticized for falling short of my mother's expectations, I grew up with an extremely diminished sense of self. I think one of the most significant aspects of my healing journey is that I finally recognized the futility of trying to get what I needed from a mother who wasn't able to provide it. I also came to realize that defining my self-worth through her eyes didn't make sense either, and came to terms with the reality that no one can make me feel lousy about myself, unless I'm a willing participant.

In order to become the person I wanted to be, I recognized that two primary changes needed to happen: I had to find ways to love myself, and I needed to let go of my painful past, refusing to let it continue to define me. In order to become visible, I needed to stop relying on validation from others, and put an end to feeling sorry for myself. To be a real presence in the world I was challenged to find ways to strengthen myself emotionally, physically and spiritually.

This initially seemed impossible, but once I made this critical shift in my thinking, the pieces of my healing journey began to come together. Once I understood that the choice to be happy was up to me, the way I viewed myself changed dramatically. When I looked at myself I now saw qualities that I really liked, and I began to build on my strengths. Eventually, I discovered this was an opportunity for significant personal growth, and that I was the one in charge. As I began to discard ghost related thoughts that didn't serve me, I discovered the power that had always existed inside of me, my spirit. In finally dealing with feelings of anger and sadness that I'd stored up since childhood, I felt much better equipped to make positive changes as an adult.

One of the issues that I had to deal with was relying too much on others to help me. It took a long time to accept that the physical ailments I was struggling with were directly related to unresolved emotions from the pain of never connecting with my mother. Since I'd been reluctant to admit what I was feeling, and didn't know what I could do about it, I had unconsciously buried these feelings deep inside; and they came back to haunt me. Most of the professionals I looked to for help also didn't make the connection that my physical problems were being caused by the emotional pain I hadn't acknowledged or dealt with.

This pattern continued for many years until I realized that I was the only person who knew all that I'd been through, and it was extremely empowering to start taking responsibility for my own physical, mental and spiritual health. I'm now going to share all that I've learned with you, including the shortcuts, how to address all aspects of your being, and a logical way of moving forward. We'll take this step by step; I'll show you what works, and how to make healing from a ghost mother a reality in your life. These ghost-busting strategies provide a *complete blueprint* that will show you how to build a foundation to repair your pain, and provide a variety of tools and techniques to work with. You get to choose which tools to use, and how far you want to go in your healing journey. By doing the exercises at the end of each chapter, you have already sampled some of the approaches; as you work through these steps, continue to identify and refine which ones are most effective and appealing to you.

Numerous exercises and techniques are introduced as part of this blueprint. The intention is not to overwhelm you, and the expectation is not that you do all of them. The breadth of information offered is to ensure that your style of healing is addressed, and to present new healing tools you may not know about, or haven't viewed as being a helpful approach in healing from a ghost mother.

Introducing 6 Ghost-Busting Strategies to Accelerate Your Healing

The six steps: **Recognize, Release, Refocus, Restore, Renovate, and Rewrite**, are presented in a sequence that takes you through the entire healing process. The importance of each step is explained, then self-help strategies are introduced; strategies you can implement right away. I've included additional techniques to further enhance your progress, and there's a **Recommended Resources** section at the end of the book that lists all the recommended techniques and resources.

In working through the steps you'll find that your energy and mood begin to shift in substantial ways, from being negatively engaged with the pain of your past, to identifying the personal power that is always available to you.

These are important **YES Statements!** to help get you focused, and "psyched up" for the healing journey ahead. Say each one out loud before you get started:

- **YES! I didn't get what I needed growing up.**
- **YES! I can release my feelings related to this pain.**
- **YES! I get to choose whether to hold onto the lessons I've learned.**
- **YES! I've taken on my mother's pain, and I can let it go.**
- **YES! I can get what I need and deserve by nurturing my own spirit.**

STEP #1

RECOGNIZE the reality of your past, and what your ghost mother can't provide.

Primary Goal: Recognize that there are limitations to what you can get from a ghost mother, but there's no limit to what you can do for yourself.

The importance of this step: In this initial step you'll come to terms with your ghost mother relationship as it really is, not as you want it to be. You've already gotten all that she has to give, continuing to long for more means missing out on your own life. Letting go of this longing provides the freedom to get your needs met in ways that work. Put an end to the pattern of chasing, as you are the person best positioned to create the changes you want in your life. Your ghost mother continues to have power over you because of your belief that she has something you need. When you recognize that she doesn't, her power dissipates, and your power begins to come into focus.

EXERCISE: This exercise helps re-define your mother's role in your life.

We're going to explore how you currently define your relationship with your mother, and replace this with a new definition. This exercise is an essential part of your healing journey. Find a quiet place where you can focus, give yourself plenty of time, and be prepared to write notes about this experience in your journal.

PART ONE: Picture the current relationship with your mother.

1. Write a list that describes the nurturing you've needed from your mother, to include: unconditional love, acceptance, validation, listening, empathy, concern, kindness, guidance, etc.

2. Take 3 slow, deep breaths. Then repeat each of the statements below, until you begin to experience an emotional or physical response. Pay attention to what you feel in your body, and the thoughts that come to you. After sitting with this for as long as needed, write down in your journal all the

thoughts, physical sensations, and emotions that came up for you.

Repeat each statement:

- *My mother is someone who doesn't give me what I need.*
- *I need to try harder to get what I need from her.*
- *Deep inside my mother must love me, why don't I feel loved by her?*

PART TWO: Picture a new relationship with your mother.

1. Now work through the next set of statements, doing so in the same way. This begins to replace your sense of longing with new messages that focus on accepting your ghost mother as she is, and helps replace your sense of longing with a healthier perspective.

   - *My mother is a ghost. Her illusiveness is caused by her personal pain and problems.*
   - *I didn't cause my mother's pain, and I can't fix it.*

- *My mother is unable to connect with me at an emotional level.*
- *I release myself from my mother's suffering, in order to end my own.*

2. Try to stick with this exercise until your emotions, and your body, begin to settle down. Repeat all the steps over a period of days, or longer. Allow yourself to feel the pain this elicits within you, comforted by the knowledge that doing so is an important part of moving beyond these difficult feelings.

IMPORTANT NOTE: *If the intensity of your emotions takes you by surprise, if you find that accessing them feels overwhelming, or makes it difficult for you to continue with the daily tasks of your life, I strongly encourage you to elicit the help of a professional to provide guidance in working through this pain.*

ADDITIONAL SELF-HELP STRATEGIES TO RECOGNIZE YOUR REALITY.

Utilize the power of positive affirmations.

These simple statements trigger the subconscious mind in amazing ways. Clarify what you want, then create positive statements to be repeated several times daily. Examples: *I can easily get my needs met. I have the ability within me to be nurtured. I know what I need, and can find ways to receive it.* Affirmations are simple, proven, powerful ways to implement change.

Learn more about your mother's illusiveness.

If you have some insight in this regard, find ways to educate yourself about her problems. Do so to increase *your* insight and knowledge, not with the intention of confronting, or trying to fix her.

Create a needs list.

Actively identify what your needs are by writing down whatever comes to mind: acceptance, caring, accomplishment, freedom, etc. Add to this list as more needs occur to you. This will help clarify your needs so that your subconscious mind starts to find ways to meet them, and will increase awareness of what additional action steps are needed.

Treat yourself with kindness and compassion.

Beginning today, do at least two nice things for yourself daily such as: *making a positive self-statement, sipping a soothing cup of tea, taking a walk in the park, getting a massage, slipping into a hot bubble-bath.*

ADDITIONAL RECOMMENDED TECHNIQUES AND RESOURCES FOR THIS GOAL.

Read the book: *You Can Heal Your Life.*
This book, by Louise Hay, provides excellent information on how "mental work" can be used to create positive healing, including exploration of the affirmations she embraced in healing from serious childhood trauma.

Don't go it alone.
Dealing with ghost mother issues can bring up a considerable amount of emotional pain that can feel overwhelming. Your ability to move forward can be enhanced by getting help from someone trained in the complexities of human behavior, someone who understands what you are trying to achieve. Ask friends, your health care provider, or search professional organizations online for referrals to qualified helping professionals in your area.

Read the book: *Will I Ever Be Good Enough?*
If your ghost mother has narcissistic qualities, this book by Dr. Karyl McBride provides great insight and is extremely helpful, particularly Part Three, which focuses on a model for recovery.

Focus on feeling thankful.

Start to keep a *gratitude journal* in which you write down the people, events, and opportunities that you are grateful for on a daily basis. Focusing on what you appreciate is uplifting, and puts the focus on creating even more in your life to be grateful for.

STEP #2

RELEASE the pain that creates negative emotions, and damages your spirit.

Primary goal: To move past the pain of a ghost mother by letting go of the toxic emotions that are stuck in your mind and body.

The importance of this step: In this step you'll learn how to release painful thoughts and feelings that are connected to the experience of being raised by a ghost mother. To do so requires exploring ways to let go of the *emotional baggage* you've been carrying around that is detrimental to your emotional, physical, and spiritual health. These strategies will help you reduce the repressed pain that's been created over time in dealing with your ghost mother. This doesn't mean you have to revisit all the painful moments you've experienced; it does mean making a conscious decision to release these negative emotions.

EXERCISE: This exercise helps release the negative emotions that you've repressed, or inappropriately expressed.

We're going to identify the emotions you need to release, and the most effective ways to do so. This is an essential part of your healing, one that has to happen before you can successfully move forward. Set aside plenty of time to work through this exercise, and jot down notes in your journal.

PART ONE: Identify negative emotions that need to be released.

1. Close your eyes. Ask yourself this question: *What painful emotions am I holding on to, related to growing up with a ghost mother?* Sit quietly and focus on this question, repeat it as many times as needed. If the question doesn't elicit any response over time, focus on bringing into your awareness a specific incident with your mother. Note the emotions that come up as you re-play the incident in your mind.

2. Sit with the emotions as long as you're able to do so. Pay attention to whatever you feel,

think, or experience in your body, and try to assign an emotion to it. Sadness, grief, anger, outrage, and fear are emotions that often come up; there are many more you may experience.

PART TWO: Releasing the negative emotions.

1. Now open your eyes. Write, or draw, on a piece of paper each negative emotion you became aware of while doing the exercise. Don't think about what you're expressing, just work with whatever comes into your mind. Make no judgments, and take your time.

2. Then create a ritual to literally let go of the emotions you've excavated, and now want to get rid of. Spend some time looking at each piece of paper you create, and then find a way to release the emotion that no longer serves you. Here are a few ideas:

- Safely burn each piece of paper; fire is a powerful way of letting go.
- Tear up each piece of paper, as you verbally express your pleasure in doing so.
- Write or draw a brief comment about each emotion on a balloon with a marker.
- Release the balloon into the sky, and watch until it becomes a tiny speck.

ADDITIONAL SELF-HELP STRATEGIES TO RELEASE YOUR PAIN.

Listen to music that moves.
Music helps to elicit and express emotion. This works particularly well with anger. Find a song that brings up feelings for you, then dance, stomp around, sing loudly, or find other ways to release negative emotions along with the music.

Focus on physical activity.
Encouraging the physical release of negative emotions is very effective for most people. Connect with difficult feelings while you are physically active, to include running, swimming, dancing, or walking briskly. Hit a punching bag, beat up a pillow, or hit your bed with a plastic bat.

Use mental imagery.
Close your eyes. Picture the emotions that are stuck inside your body by picturing the events that created them, or naming various emotions out loud. Now focus on moving the negative energy out of your body, either through the top of your head, or out through your arms. Shake your arms for a few minutes as you complete this exercise, in order to further release pent up emotions.

Just breathe.
Set aside time each day during which you focus on paying attention to your breath as it moves in and out of your body.

If your mind wanders, simply notice this and bring your attention back to the breath. This meditative practice helps quiet the mind in important ways. If an emotion comes up, notice it and then let it out with the next exhalation.

ADDITIONAL RECOMMENDED TECHNIQUES AND RESOURCES FOR THIS GOAL.

Learn about EFT.

Emotional Freedom Techniques increasingly are being used as an effective way to apply a sequence of easily learned *tapping* techniques to interrupt negative emotional patterns. It's best to learn this simple technique from someone trained in this process, but it's also possible to learn, and use, the techniques on your own.

Develop a mind-body practice.

Participating in these practices is soothing to the mind and body, and helps in releasing the blockages that develop as a result of suppressing painful emotions. Find the one that's right for you, there are different styles within each practice:

> **Yoga:** a series of poses with emphasis on paying attention to the breath.
>
> **Tai Chi:** exercises performed in a slow, relaxed sequence.
>
> **Qigong:** combines breathing with energy control through slow, specific movements.

Listen to the CD: *Anger Releasing.*

This wonderful CD developed by Louise Hay uses imagery and other techniques that take you through a process of identifying, and letting go of what's contributing to your angry feelings. This can be repeated as many times as needed, or can be done with the support of a therapist, or other helping professional.

Experience laughter yoga.

As the saying goes, laughter is the best medicine. The physical and emotional benefits of laughing include the release of negative emotions, and the production of feel-good chemicals in the body. If you have difficulty finding something that makes you laugh, check out a Laughter Yoga class in which laughter is replicated in a body exercise, and then turns into the real thing.

STEP #3

REFOCUS on developing a strong identity that allows you to get your needs met.

Primary goal: As you develop your own identity, viewing yourself as worthwhile and deserving of happiness, your sense of inner power will dramatically increase.

The importance of this step: Moving past the pain requires learning to love yourself, which doesn't happen easily when you've spent so much of your life focusing on someone else, and feeling unlovable. Self-esteem normally develops as we grow up, through the attention and feedback provided by our parents. What's needed now is to focus on re-defining your value as a person, and insisting that you view yourself in positive terms.

EXERCISE: This exercise is designed to teach you to talk back to your inner-critic.

We're going to make the very believable assumption that your self-esteem has been badly damaged during the process of being raised by a ghost mother. Repairing the damage requires exploring how you've internalized the negative messages, either coming to believe them, or not yet having challenged them. Carve out a period of time when you won't be interrupted, and set up a way to record information, preferably in your journal.

1. Find a quiet place to ponder this question. *What are the qualities that I most admire in others?* Try to come up with at least 5 personal qualities that you consider important, such as: brave, trustworthy, responsible, kind, loving, dependable.

2. Consider each quality one at a time, and ask yourself: *Is this a quality that I possess?* Answer YES or NO to each of the qualities identified.

3. As you consider how each of these desirable qualities apply to you, listen to the critical self-talk that will most likely emerge. Pay attention to what happens when, for example, you ask yourself: *Can I be trusted? Am I brave? Do others see me as loving?*

4. What you're looking for is the *inner-critic*, the harsh self-talk, the ways you beat yourself up with negative comments you may not even be aware of. Listen for the responses that come to mind, with the intention of starting to identify how you verbally talk to and mistreat yourself.

5. You may need to repeat this process over a period of time in order to get a better view of how your inner-critic talks to you. You may even come up with a name for her. Does she work alone, or is there a *critical committee* within you? Humor can certainly help in uncovering these negative thought patterns.

6. The more you pay attention to your inner-critic, the easier it becomes to manage her. When she speaks, it's best to listen without judgment. Question the validity of this negative chatter, and begin to replace it with positive thoughts and statements.

ADDITIONAL SELF-HELP STRATEGIES TO REFOCUS ON YOUR IDENTITY.

Focus on who you want to be.
Identify statements that encourage a positive self-image such as: *I like who I am. I have a beautiful spirit. I feel good about myself.* These powerful messages are very effective in reversing a negative self-image. Write down your positive statements, and post a list where you'll see them often.

Make a powerful list.
Create a list that identifies all your positive qualities: courage, determination, generosity, kindness, etc. Add to this list on an ongoing basis as you increasingly pay attention to what you like, and love, about yourself. Remember to review this list daily.

Create an exercise routine.
Movement makes us feel better. Do what you enjoy, aiming for at least 10 minutes daily. Walking, running, grooving to the music, it all works in making a difference in how you feel. An added benefit is that following through on personal goals helps to improve your self-esteem.

Consider others.
Perform random acts of kindness in which you do something kind for someone else, without any expectation of thanks, or acknowledgement. This contributes to feeling good about you, and decreases dependence on needing validation from others.

ADDITIONAL RECOMMENDED TECHNIQUES AND RESOURCES FOR THIS GOAL.

Learn from a CD on self-esteem.
Carolyn Myss, an intuitive healer, has created a highly recommended CD titled: **Self-Esteem: Your Fundamental Power.** She defines self-esteem as an essential power that impacts all aspects of our lives. The information includes exercises to strengthen and improve your sense of self, and discusses how doing so improves your ability to heal.

Read about ways to feel better.
Self-esteem: A Proven Program of Cognitive Techniques for Assessing, Improving and Maintaining Your Self-Esteem, written by Matthew McKay PhD, and Patrick Fanning provides techniques for understanding and enhancing self-esteem.

Consider yoga therapy.
Yoga therapy, such as *Phoenix Rising,* uses basic yoga postures, and breath work with assistance from a professional instructor, to help make connections between the mind and body, which contributes to an increased sense of well-being. Guidance is provided on how to release negative emotions effectively. No prior yoga experience is required to benefit from this method. Another way to explore these concepts is through the CD: **Yoga for Emotional Flow**, by Stephen Cope.

Try EMDR, a therapeutic technique.

Eye Movement Desensitization and Reprocessing is a proven technique to help reduce trauma through eye movements that encourage the brain to process painful memories differently. The memories are still there, but they are less vivid and upsetting.

STEP #4

RESTORE your confidence, emotional strength and self-knowledge.

Primary goal: Continue to improve how you view yourself in order to increase your ability to access your inner strength, and trust your intuition.

The importance of this step: This step further enhances your healing by encouraging the development of your personal power, and intuition. Learning to focus on nurturing, compassionate thoughts shifts how you think about yourself and what you're capable of, in addition to improving your mood and energy. This step is designed to increase your self-understanding, so that you come to appreciate who you are, and how you relate to others. Sometimes we believe that what we think about in the privacy of our minds isn't important, but nothing could be further from the truth. Our thoughts and internal dialogue have a significant impact on our body, mind and spirit.

EXERCISE: The purpose of this exercise is to develop compassionate language for your internal dialogue.

The previous exercise increased your awareness of negative self-talk. This exercise introduces tools to treat yourself in kinder, gentler ways, so you don't continue the pattern of abusing yourself, to include internal dialogue that is blaming and judgmental. Give yourself plenty of time to work through these concepts, they are very important in creating a new perspective in which you view, and think about yourself as someone who is worthwhile, and deserving of happiness. This shift provides the essence of what it takes to live a visible life.

1. Imagine that you've done, or said, something you don't feel good about. Let's use this example: *You've just slammed down the phone during a conversation with your sister in which you became angry in response to her demeaning comments about your husband.* You recognize she was out of line, but after

making this impulsive decision you feel angry, guilty and ashamed of yourself.

2. Let's assume that in response to this incident you immediately make the following comment to yourself: *I really blew it; I'm such a jerk. I don't know why she puts up with me.* Now brainstorm ways to think differently about this action and your response to it, using language and concepts that are more empowering—and probably more accurate.

3. Come up with at least 2 different ways of "talking" to yourself for each of the questions below.

   - *How would you phrase your comment if you were talking to someone else?*
   - *Is it possible to question your behavior without making such harsh generalizations?*
   - *If you wanted to feel loved and cared about, what would you say?*
   - *How would you respond if you knew someone else was listening?*

4. Here are a few suggested kind, compassionate responses to the example: *I may have over reacted; I need some time to think about this. I was really upset by her comments, and didn't know what to say. I love myself, and handled this the best way I knew how.*

5. You may be surprised at the difference it can make to treat yourself with respect, love and kindness. Think about this quote from Buddha, in considering future responses: ***You yourself, as much as anybody in the Universe, deserve your love and affection.***

6. Write up a summary of what you've learned in your journal. The intention of this exercise is not to say that you don't need to hold yourself accountable for your actions, you do, but in ways that don't repeat abusive patterns, and are instead, loving and supportive.

SELF-HELP STRATEGIES TO RESTORE YOUR INNER STRENGTH.

Listen to a music CD.
Songs for the Inner Child, by Shaina Noll includes songs such as: *Deep Peace, How Could Anyone.* These soothing lullabies are designed for those who weren't nurtured as children. They are calming to listen to, and provide healing at a deep level.

Consider this question.
You may be haunted by internalized messages that suggest you can't become happier, or accomplish more, than your ghost mother. This message may be outside of your conscious awareness, but can strongly impact behavior. Sit quietly and ask yourself this: *Does it make me uncomfortable to achieve more than my mother has?* Pay close attention to your reactions in response to this question in order to determine if this is a roadblock to getting what you want.

Reduce the critical chatter.
Begin to notice the critical self-talk that pops into your mind throughout the day. Pay particular attention to the negative messages that come up when you make a mistake, can't make a decision, or feel stressed, as these are the times when negative messages are most likely to emerge. When a critical thought comes up, don't judge it; replace it with a compassionate one. Or, try repeating the simple chant *Om Shanti* (which means peace) as a way to help calm the internal chatter.

Adopt a friend.

Consider adopting a furry pet that will provide you unconditional love. Research supports the value of animal companionship in human healing. Perhaps "rescue" and bring home an adorable, engaging dog, cat or bunny.

ADDITIONAL RECOMMENDED TECHNIQUES AND RESOURCES FOR THIS GOAL.

Create a shield of protection.

Protect yourself from hurtful or upsetting comments made by others by visualizing a shield made of hard plastic that wraps around you. Negative comments will not be able to penetrate this barrier, and help to protect your emerging sense of self. A great source for ideas about shielding, setting boundaries etc. is explained in the book: **Whose Life is it Anyway? By Nina W. Brown.**

Try acupuncture.

Many people don't realize the *emotional benefits* of this system of Chinese Medicine that's been practiced for thousands of years, and has well-documented, positive results. In addition to providing relief from physical pain, it can also be used to help relieve emotional pain, including depression and anxiety, helping you to strengthen yourself from the inside out.

Explore the benefits of CBT.

Cognitive-Behavioral Therapy describes various therapy techniques that focus on understanding, and working with the critical connection between thoughts, feelings and behaviors. Increasingly this approach is receiving acclaim for providing short-term solutions to specific problems in which a person feels emotionally stuck.

Get support in a CoDA group.

Co-Dependents Anonymous is a support group for anyone seeking healthy, loving relationships, through the 12-step philosophy that has helped many people.

STEP #5

RENOVATE your life, and your perception of yourself in powerful ways.

Primary goal: To come to terms with how you were negatively impacted by your ghost mother, and to strengthen your mental toughness so that you do NOT see yourself as a victim.

The importance of this step: is to accept yourself, and your past, at a deep level of understanding. You now get to make choices about the perspective in which you view your past; keeping in mind that this will strongly impact your future. You are going to clear out *the emotional clutter* in order to take charge of every aspect of your life. It is your choice now: whether to use the pain of your past in constructive ways that create positive change, or in destructive ways that repeat abusive patterns, or provide an excuse not to move forward.

Continuing to view yourself as a victim creates a sense of powerlessness within you, and keeps you stuck repeating negative patterns. In reality, you're a survivor who has leaped over huge obstacles in order to get where you are today. Being a victim suggests being deeply wounded, injured, suffering. Being a survivor suggests the opposite—enduring, carrying on, staying alive.

EXERCISE: This exercise allows you to experience the profound shift in energy that occurs when you no longer define yourself as a victim, but instead view yourself as a strong survivor.

1. Close your eyes. Picture yourself as someone who has been victimized by the way she grew up. See yourself as having almost no power over your own life. Feel sad about your circumstances, and certain that your situation can never improve. Sit with this image of yourself for as long as possible, at least several minutes.

2. Now think about, and write down your responses to the following questions:

   • *What's the strongest emotion you're feeling right now?*
   • *Are you feeling resentment or anger towards your mother?*
   • *Do you feel capable of doing anything you want to do?*
   • *Are you filled with a sense of gratitude?*
   • *What does your body feel like right now?*

3. Breathe in slowly through your nose while counting to 5, hold for the count of 2, and slowly release while counting to 5. Repeat.

4. Now picture yourself as a strong woman, a survivor. In spite of the obstacles of growing up with a ghost mother, you have demonstrated incredible courage, and a strong belief in better things to come. Say out loud: *I am not a victim; this has not destroyed me. I've learned about myself, and how powerful I really am. The past is behind me.*

5. Pay close attention to the difference in your energy, thoughts, and how your body feels as compared to a few minutes ago when you were in victim-mode. Answer the same

   questions as before, and note the difference in your answers.

   • *What's the strongest emotion you're feeling right now?*
   • *Are you feeling resentment or anger towards your mother?*
   • *Do you feel capable of doing anything you want to do?*
   • *Are you filled with a sense of gratitude?*
   • *What does your body feel like right now?*

6. In your journal, write about the differences in these two perspectives, and how it felt to shift from one to the other. For most women, this is an important lesson in their ability to positively influence thoughts and feelings.

SELF-HELP STRATEGIES TO RENOVATE YOUR LIFE.

Renovate your thoughts.

Pay attention to thoughts of self-pity that come up for you such as: *I didn't get what other people got from their mother. Why do I have to work so hard at growing up?* When such thoughts emerge, respond with different thoughts that acknowledge everything you do have to be grateful for.

Acknowledge your strengths.

Literally pat yourself on the back to acknowledge the courage it's taken for you to survive being raised by a ghost mother. Pay attention daily, and give yourself credit for the many skills you've developed in coping with this pain.

Try this restorative pose.

Child's Pose is a simple pose that quickly calms the brain and body. It's an excellent way to bring a sense of balance into your life, within a matter of minutes.

1. Kneel on the floor, with your knees separated.
2. Slowly stretch forward until your forehead is on the floor, use a pillow if needed.
3. You can rest with your arms stretched forward in front of your head, or bring your arms back, and rest them by your sides.

Learn from your anger.

Read and work through the intriguing book: **The Dance of Anger:** *A Woman's Guide to Changing the Patterns of Intimate Relationships,* by Harriet Lerner, Ph.D., a guide to identifying angry feelings that explores effective ways to view anger as a tool you can work with. To quote the author, "Anger is a signal, and one worth listening to."

ADDITIONAL recommended techniques and resources for this goal.

Try hypnosis.

Hypnosis is a therapeutic technique that establishes a deep sense of relaxation. Healers trained in this technique can help you gain a greater understanding of your subconscious mind which is very valuable in changing thoughts, and behavior patterns.

Get help with forgiving.

Dr. Carolle Jean-Murat has written an interactive workbook about forgiveness that is very helpful, and can be downloaded immediately from her website. Here is an exercise she has developed in order to work on forgiving yourself:

1. Write down everything you are ashamed of.
2. Write down everything you feel guilty about.
3. Write a letter to yourself saying that you forgive yourself for all of it.

4. Write another letter to yourself about all the wonderful qualities you have, and all that you do for others. This is called a "Gratitude Letter to Yourself." It's not about ego, but about recognizing that you are a person of value and worth, and that you bring meaning to the lives of others. This, in turn, gives your own life more meaning and depth.

Learn ways to relieve stress.

Relaxation techniques help to calm your nervous system, and your body, making it easier to tune into your real thoughts, and access your inner wisdom. The CD **Letting Go of Stress**, by Emmett Miller, M.D., and Steven Halpern presents four simple and effective relaxation methods that will help identify the approach that works best for you. All you have to do is close your eyes and follow the simple instructions.

Develop a meditation practice.

Explore ways to meditate by participating in a class, or listening to a CD such as: **Guided Mindfulness Meditation** by Jon Kabat-Zinn. The practice of meditation has a variety of benefits to help you heal and feel better, to include calming your nervous system, helping you think more clearly, accessing your intuition, and for some, tapping into the existence of a higher power.

STEP #6

REWRITE a new life-script by using the hidden gifts of being raised by a ghost mother.

Primary goal: To have a future filled with joy and peace as you continue to move forward with a strong sense of gratitude, and personal power.

The importance of this step: Now it's time to combine all of the insights, and information gained from working through the previous ghost-busting steps to come to terms with your mother's illusiveness, and enhance your inner sense of power and purpose. It's time to make plans for yourself, and your future, as you rewrite your past by focusing on the constructive, informative, compassionate aspects of all that you've learned.

Living in the past isn't where you want to be; your power is in the present. This final step will propel you into a new way of living that is more real than anything you've encountered before. As a child, you frequently didn't play an important role in your own life-story, but now you will create stories in which you are a heroine, with super-powers. Come to think of it, you can write your new story to include anything you want! This healing work creates the freedom to revisit your story with considerably less pain and misery, and if you can include a few details of how you've actually benefited from the experience, then so much the better.

EXERCISE: this is an exercise that allows you to experience what empowerment feels like.

1. To get the most from this exercise, initially spend time outside in a place that's inspiring for you. Perhaps you prefer sparkling water, lush trees, or snow-capped mountains. In this setting, wander around for a while, using all your senses to make a connection with the outdoors, and to appreciate all that nature has to offer. This is always accessible to you; there is energy in nature that can always nourish your spirit.

2. Make a decision about whether to do the rest of the exercise outside, or to return to an indoor setting.

3. This is an easy sequence to learn and remember, look over the instructions now.

    Stand up straight and tall, with your arms by your side.

    Cross your wrists gently in front of you, now inhale slowly as you gently bring your arms upward, until they are above your head.

    Raise your chin slightly.

    Hold this position, and your breath, for a period of time that's comfortable for you.

Now slowly release your breath as you bring both arms back down to your sides.

Repeat this sequence several times, using your own initiative to add as much stretching as you like, and to notice that at one point during the sequence you are reaching up to the heavens.

4. This is a liberating, empowering pose for the body, mind and spirit, the perfect way to start each morning. Repeat the sequence for as long as you like, and note *all* the sensations that emerge while you are doing so.

5. To add even more to this experience, use the following statements. Think about each one during your inhale. Then release your breath with a strong exhale, as you slowly return your arms to your sides.

   - *I grew up with a challenging reality.*
   - *It no longer haunts me.*
   - *I now focus on all that I've learned.*
   - *I release what doesn't serve me.*
   - *I am in charge of my own destiny.*

6. Allow yourself to feel and think about the impact of this experience, and make follow-up notes in your journal.

SELF-HELP STRATEGIES TO REWRITE YOUR SCRIPT.

Reframe your experience.

Use the therapeutic technique of reframing, which means viewing past experiences through a different lens, one that now sees the same experience in different ways. For example: *Having a ghost mother has helped me learn how to nurture myself. In dealing with this I've learned how determined I am.*

Dream.

Pay attention to your dreams, those you have during the night, and during the day. This is your unconscious at work, revealing clues about what's most important to you, and possible ways to achieve what you desire. Write them all down. Keep paper, or a recording device, by your bed to capture your dreams while you still remember them. Then record them in your journal.

Design a plan.

Research shows that written goals are far more likely to be met than ones you just think about. Take a page from what every entrepreneur knows; it's critical to develop a detailed plan. Design yours to include hopes and dreams for the future, greatly increasing the odds that you will succeed.

Visualize the new you.

Close your eyes and visualize yourself as the visible, content person you want to be. Pay attention to the details, to include what you say to yourself, and your viewpoint towards yourself, and others. Think of this as a *dress rehearsal,* a way to identify and practice new ways of thinking, feeling and being. Not only will this practice help identify your true desires, it will also set into motion getting what you want because the mind can't differentiate between what you visualize, and what you actually experience—such is the power of picturing yourself as an empowered person.

ADDITIONAL RECOMMENDED TECHNIQUES AND RESOURCES FOR THIS GOAL.

Open up to this book.
Read the intriguing book: **Legacy of the Heart:** *The Spiritual Advantages of a Painful Childhood,* by Wayne Muller, which describes the unique wisdom that can develop from this pain, and will help you look at your past from a very different perspective.

Take time for joy and laughter.
Growing up with a ghost mother can wring the joy from life. Bring it back by taking the time to do what makes you happy, and to find humor in day-to-day living. One way to "wake up with a smile" is to enjoy the simple wisdom and laughter contained in the book: **Are You As Happy As Your Dog?** by Alan Cohen.

Participate in an Aikido class.

This powerful form of Japanese martial arts teaches techniques to center the mind and body using moves that require little physical strength. Aikido translates as "the way of harmony of the spirit," and can provide physical, mental and emotional healing as it focuses on *blending* with the energy of your opponent, rather than resisting or opposing it.

Consider a new spiritual perspective.

Increase your understanding of spiritual principles and practices by reading Reverend Wendy Craig-Purcell's enlightening book: **Ask Yourself This: *Questions to Open the Heart, Expand the Mind and Awaken the Soul.***

A Quick Summary of Ghost-Busting Concepts

- You are not defined by your past, live in the present.

- Stop chasing your ghost mother.

- Accept the pain of growing up ghost mothered; then embrace the rest of your life.

- Know that you aren't alone.

- Focus on all aspects of your healing: emotional, physical and spiritual.

- The problems in your life that keep repeating point to unresolved ghost issues.

- Seek professional support to work through intense emotions.

- Reclaim your power by taking responsibility for the choices you make.

- Choose not to see yourself as a victim.

- **This journey is ultimately not about your mother; it's about you.**

- **Your healing journey has the potential to teach amazing lessons.**

- **It's important to speak the truth of your experience.**

- **Embrace yourself in order to let go of the past, and then rewrite your life.**

Ending the Legacy of the Ghost Mother

Can the legacy that's created by a ghost mother be ended? I'm certain that it can. In finding the courage to share your story, in developing compassion for yourself, and refusing to live in the shadow of a ghost mother, you *can* create a different way of living, and a much more powerful way of being in the world. In embracing your truth, you'll come to see what you did receive from your ghost mother, and actively work on getting for yourself what you will never receive from her.

As you continue to deal with ghost issues ask yourself if you are responding to interactions with your mother in the present, or in the past? Are you linking your current experience with past memories, or being impacted by what you previously didn't get from her? Try to make these connections, and to deal only with what is a real issue *in the present*. Healing from a ghost mother requires the willingness to change your perceptions, thoughts, and feelings to accurately reflect reality, and to take responsibility for moving forward.

I asked the women who've shared their stories throughout this book to discuss what they've learned in their efforts to heal from a ghost mother, and to offer some advice. Here are their comments:

Lynne:

The advice I can offer someone trying to come to terms with a ghost mother is this, believe and trust that everyone in life has a purpose, simply by being alive. We each have our own individual path in life to explore, to include deserved happiness, and even with detours from this path there can be learning experiences in managing life better. A ghost mother has her own path, and it is separate from yours; one path is not better than the other, they are just different. Accepting your mother, whether you like her, agree with her, or understand her, is the key.

Advocate for yourself. Cherish your own wonderful qualities, daily. Re-evaluate and diversify your support system if necessary. Manage your own path by deciding what to allow into your life that feels healthy, and safe. Then create boundaries to support your vision, if you don't do this, then who will? Ghost mothers don't have the ability to do this for their daughters. Don't view yourself through her perspective; instead view yourself through your own perspective, which is the only way to become who you truly want to be.

Michelle:

The best advice I can give someone dealing with a ghost mother is to practice self-care, and to set and adhere to good boundaries. By self-care I'm referring to doing what helps you to relax, cope and take care of your own needs. I know that I no longer need to care for my mother by doing all the cooking and cleaning, while reassuring her that she's perfect. Now, I take more time to explore hobbies, and pursue interests that I was never allowed to do as a child. I no longer ask, nor need permission, to just be myself; this has been a wonderful realization!

If you need to ask for help, that's okay. I've learned it's acceptable, even good, to ask for help before I get emotionally overwhelmed. There is no longer shame associated with feeling imperfect, because I know now that I can't do everything by myself. It's been very helpful to attend support groups to work on my issues with codependency, it's also helped me to read positive books, focus on my spirituality with God, and do daily self-affirmations. I think it's about what works best for each individual, there's no right or wrong way to take care of yourself. It takes time, but for me, life has gotten much better.

Susan:

To answer the question, "How am I healing?" I share the following: I'm trying to please myself more, to understand what is right for me, and to reduce the inordinately high need to please others at the expense of myself. I have worked much harder to create boundaries, by setting limits regarding exactly what I am willing to do, and when I can do it. I've learned to let go of the need for my mother's validation, knowing now that my happiness cannot be tied to the approval of someone who doesn't have the capacity to give it. I'm learning to change maladaptive behaviors that constrict and impede me.

Writing is therapeutic for me; I usually write when I am really "pissed off," it's a way to vent my feelings. I have done a good job of letting go of feeling responsible for my mother. For me, healing is an emotional roller coaster that involves gradual change; it is easy to become impatient. I have a broad range of friends, some are mother figures, and all of them love me for who I am. I've learned that you don't have to love your mother even though a lot of people may think you do (they don't know your story). I have to work on myself every day, but I'm in a much better place today because of the work I do, the wonderful friends I have, and my own initiative.

Jody:

Be your own independent adult. List your accomplishments such as, "I bought a house, a car, got an education." Keep the list going. Think about how far you've come in life to be where you are now. Ask yourself, "What do I think?" whenever you are making a decision. Also, find ways to learn that you are a good, loving, compassionate and kind person, because being good and kind is what really matters in life. Love and kindness is what life is all about, so you've got all that it takes. Your good character is all that is needed to be accepted and respected by others; this was a total shock to me, that life is not all about serving Mom and trying to get her approval.

Stand up to them. Ghosts aren't as scary when you get logical and fight back. It helps to step back from your mother, and to realize that you can't have an intimate and trustworthy relationship with her. I'm going to just appreciate who I am today, and thank God I'm not a ghost, and that I can heal. I feel that I'm still in the process of healing.

Tanya:

I'm new in my understanding of this situation. I'm in therapy, and trying to find new ways to deal with my painful feelings, especially anger. Let me tell you that I no longer allow anyone to push me around in any way, not emotionally, physically or spiritually. It's vital to me to be in control of as much of my own life as possible. I'm certainly more in touch with my feelings now. I'm learning to say, "I feel-I want" in expressing myself to others, especially my husband. It's hard for me because for most of my life, I've taken care of everyone but myself.

I think it's important to realize the problems that your mother has, and find out more about them, if possible. I realize that for all these years I've been trying to get blood from a stone. Now that you know she's illusive, how do you deal with it? How much relationship do you allow between yourself and your ghost mother? What about siblings, will they understand, or deny? You may need to completely distance yourself from her. Each of us has to decide what actions are best, in order to achieve peace and quiet in our lives. I can guarantee it won't be easy, but finding ways to free yourself is very necessary in order to heal.

In my own healing journey, I've learned that this process is similar to untying a tight knot, whether it's a rope, piece of string, or a delicate necklace. Often the process of un-tangling is a frustrating one, and there are times of uncertainty about whether or not you will succeed. But, when that last piece finally slips out of the knot, it is a liberating, exciting, joyous feeling. Healing from the legacy of a ghost mother is an opportunity to enrich yourself, and to take a different direction, one in which you no longer chase an illusive presence. No matter what your age, or current situation, it's never too late to become visible in your own life, to get what you need, and deserve.

It's time now to grab hold of your future, by learning from the past. Yes, your mother was an illusive presence, but you've come to see how important it is to be real. You now get to decide what you need and how to get it; you get to decide what's important, and what isn't. In working through this process, you will develop the power to move past this lack of mothering, and to live a deep, rich, fulfilling life. There *is* a light at the end of the tunnel, and it is one well worth striving for—your life can be very different than currently seems possible. Feeling happy after being raised by a ghost mother is a choice, and it's one that you get to make.

~The Journey, by Mary Oliver~

One day you finally knew,
what you had to do, and began,
though the voices around you
kept shouting
their bad advice—
Though the whole house began to tremble
and you felt the old tug at your ankles.
"Mend my life!"
each voice cried.
But you didn't stop.
You knew what you had to do,
though the wind pried with its stiff fingers
at the very foundations,
though their melancholy
was terrible.
It was already late
enough, and a wild night,
and the road full of fallen
branches and stones.
But little by little,
as you left their voices behind,
The stars began to burn
through the sheets of clouds,
and there was a new voice
which you slowly

recognized as your own,
that kept you company
as you strode deeper and deeper
into the world,
determined to do
the only thing you could do—
determined to save
the only life you could save.

CHAPTER 7

HAUNTED NO MORE

The hidden gifts of being raised by a ghost.

It isn't where you came from; it's where you're going that counts.

~ Ella Fitzgerald

Dealing With Ghosts: Further Reflections on Healing

Now that you've worked with some of the tools needed to heal from a ghost mother, you may have additional questions about the process of healing. I've tried to anticipate your questions by offering answers to the concerns that I've been asked about; and commenting on the worries that most women in this situation have.

1. Will my pain ever go away completely?

Being mothered by a ghost creates a significant emotional wound. The extent to which this wound heals depends on a number of factors to include how toxic your relationship was (or is), the extent of your resiliency, and for how long you pursue the process of healing. The range of responses to healing from a ghost mother vary from feeling better, but still being easily triggered by painful memories, to someone who embraces a strong spiritual practice, and accepts that this pain is part of their life journey. For most of us, the extent to which we continue to experience painful emotions as a result of being ghost mothered falls somewhere between these two extremes.

Remember that you constantly have a choice about how to deal with this wound. If you constantly scratch it, it will continue to bleed. If instead, you periodically check on it, perhaps taking time daily to rub a soothing lotion on it that encourages healing, then over time it will gradually fade, and become much less noticeable.

2. How do I know if I'm healing?

Healing doesn't happen overnight, it requires constant and consistent effort to change old patterns, and embrace new ones. I believe that healing begins the moment you acknowledge the pain of being raised by a ghost mother, and gains momentum as you recognize the need to take responsibility for living a visible life. Healing happens every time you focus on yourself rather than your mother, every time you acknowledge your inner wisdom, and with each step you take that serves your best interests.

Further progress in healing is made every time you let yourself feel what you really feel, rather than holding in these emotions. It happens every time you give yourself a break, appreciate all that you have to offer, and with each celebration of your success, no matter how small. If you've gotten this far, your healing has already begun and it will build on itself, and take you places that currently may be difficult to imagine.

3. How can I get help with my healing?

I highly recommend getting professional help in healing from this pain that goes so deep, and encompasses so much of who you are. Using these healing strategies is invaluable, but you will make progress even faster if you let someone else help you, someone who provides compassion, support, and encouragement. Committing to work on your healing, with the support of a professional who understands these issues, also means that you'll continue to make this journey a priority in your life.

Qualified help can come from a mental health professional, spiritual advisor, pastoral counselor, life coach, counselor, or anyone you trust and feel comfortable opening up to—but make sure this is someone trained in human behavior, and effective healing techniques. Assistance and support are usually most needed in the transition period when you stop chasing your ghost mother, and in releasing the painful feelings that arise in letting go of your past, but can be extremely useful throughout the healing process. If you have difficulty accessing your feelings, or if it's overwhelming to do so, working through the steps with someone who validates your pain and progress, while also providing a sense of safety and security, is highly recommended.

4. How long does it take to heal?

The best way to answer this question is to let you know that it depends on a number of factors to include: how committed you are to the process of healing, how toxic your ghost mother is, the degree of emotional support you had from other adults growing up, your personality, your strengths, and how long you've chased your mother. The amount of time healing takes isn't nearly as important as the *quality* of the healing. In other words, once you begin to grasp the need to heal from this pain, and how to do so, you will begin to feel better, and your healing will continue to build on itself in positive ways. Most women feel it's a huge relief to understand the underlying reason for their pain, and after this breakthrough, they continue to make ongoing progress.

5. Do I need to worry about taking on the qualities of a ghost mother?

It's healthy to be concerned about the possibility of taking on the illusive qualities of your mother, but this is less of a concern when you commit to embracing, and dealing with these issues. The fact that you *want* a different life for yourself means that you will most likely overcome her pain, and find your power. You do need to know that when under stress, it's more likely that you *will* regress to using the immature coping methods modeled by your mother, as mentioned by Dr. Carolle. Don't be surprised if this happens; try to pay attention to how you cope during these times as a teaching tool so that you're less likely to repeat these patterns.

In addition to healing yourself, if you become a mother I recommend reading books, and attending parenting classes to help prepare you for the challenges of child rearing, by learning the many skills needed to provide the mothering you didn't receive. If you have ignored, or not fully dealt with the pain of being raised this way, it will often come to haunt you if you do become a mother. Memories of being with her and the recognition of being inadequately mothered frequently emerge with the birth of a child, and fluctuating hormones don't help. It's at this point that fears and anxiety about doing better than she did will come to the forefront. If you've dealt with your ghost past, this will be less of an issue. The more you heal yourself, the better, more visible mother you can be for your child.

6. I'm healing now, so how do I deal with my ghost mother?

This is a tough one; in this regard working with a professional can be extremely helpful. Together you can develop and evaluate strategies to help you deal directly with your ghost mother in the present. Here are some practical suggestions that have worked well for others:

- Initially detach from her emotionally as much as possible, while you focus on healing yourself.

- Try to identify positive qualities, or contributions, no matter how small, that she is able to make.

- Know that the changes you are making will change both your perception of your mother, and what you need from her.

- Make decisions about how to deal with her based on how toxic the relationship is, and how emotionally damaging the interactions are.

- Recognize that sometimes it's more painful to try to maintain a relationship with a ghost mother than it is to let her go.

- Setting clear boundaries with a ghost mother is helpful, and often essential.

Michelle explains how doing so improved her situation:

> In regards to boundaries, I discovered that these have to be set in order to learn where our ghost mother ends, and where we begin. When I was a child, if someone asked me if I liked the color blue, I would have looked to my mother, and asked her if I liked this color. I used to feel extreme pressure to give her a key when, as an adult, I moved into different apartments over the years. This was unhealthy for me because she took advantage of having my key, and I later realized that a boundary needed to be set in this regard. One other thing that really helped was telling her that I could only talk on Sunday afternoons. Setting these boundaries has helped keep my relationship with her more manageable, and removed a lot of the drama from my life.

7. How do I deal with setbacks that occur in my healing?

Setbacks are *going to happen*, whether triggered by stress, physical illness, holidays, contact with your ghost mother, painful memories, or other factors. In fact, all healing happens in erratic ways, often with progress being made, and then a period of stagnation, or backwards movement, which can feel like a setback, but is to be expected.

Keep in mind that change is still happening even in the midst of a so-called setback, and you will soon regain the progress that was previously made. It's likely there will be times when you are painfully impacted by the ways that your ghost mothering continues to haunt you, but these are temporary feelings; you now have tools to use when this happens, and you know how to get support to keep moving forward. Thus, your painful feelings will no longer consume you as they did before, or take you as deeply into feelings of discouragement. This was once your reality, and there are still scars, but this is no longer where you chose to live.

8. What about the concept of forgiveness?

Forgiveness in dealing with a ghost mother can be a bit tricky to understand and implement. Too often it is touted as the *only* way to come to a sense of peace with someone who has wronged you. While I think forgiveness is important, my view is a bit different. No matter how troubled or illusive your ghost mother is, she is still *responsible for her actions*. She doesn't have the right to be physically, emotionally, or verbally abusive towards you, and has to be held accountable for her behavior. Unless she has some type of brain impairment that prevents her from differentiating right from wrong, she is held to the same standards that we all are, including not mistreating, or abusing anyone else.

That being said, I think the ability to forgive is an important one, but from a perspective of making a conscious decision to *come to terms with the reality of who your ghost mother is,* so that you no longer hold onto the painful emotions related to your experience with her. I think it's easy to misunderstand this concept, to think it means that your mother's lack of compassionate parenting was okay, but this is not what it means. This definition of forgiveness is about letting go, in order to heal and no longer suffer from this pain, a process that is profoundly healing.

I also think the person most in need of forgiveness in this situation is the one on the receiving end of this pain. It's common to accept the blame in dealing with a ghost mother, or to wish we'd known then what we know now. This isn't possible, of course, but it can be tempting to think we should have stopped chasing her sooner, should have figured out earlier that she's a ghost, and so on. Once you decide to release yourself from the flogging that goes along with this what-if thinking, I promise you will feel better. The healing work you are doing is designed to assist you to let go of the past, and come to terms with the fact that you weren't the cause of this pain.

Accept that your ghost mother did the best she could, even though she couldn't provide what you needed; and move on. When you choose to release the feelings associated with how you were raised, the benefit is an effective way to let go of a painful past; it's not about absolving her of responsibility in any way.

Growing up With a Ghost Mother Gives You a Unique Perspective

In reading this book you've seen that growing up with a ghost mother is an insidious problem that haunts your spirit, until it's recognized, and dealt with. The topic of ghost mothers is a scary one, but it becomes easier when you possess the tools to deal with her, and most importantly, to fully develop your own strength, and self-esteem. You may not feel quite ready to embrace the information revealed in this final chapter, but I encourage you to keep reading because of the sense of hope that this knowledge provides. As you continue to reap the benefits of healing, there's little doubt that you'll recognize the unlimited potential to learn and grow from this experience.

Perhaps you fear that the years spent chasing your mother have become a liability, but soon you'll discover that what we learn from our early illusive existence makes it possible not only to heal, but to further empower ourselves by continuing to draw on these powerful lessons. In opening to these possibilities, we are able to embrace concepts that profoundly benefit our ability to live, and to love. Healing from this pain is ultimately about not being a victim, and not blaming our mother. It's about using this experience to deepen our understanding, and appreciation for life. Learning who we are from the inside out, discovering our resiliency and capacity for change, is information that continues to encourage self-appreciation and self-discovery.

In working through my ghost pain I often had the sensation of falling into a black hole. Many of you have been there too; *it's a place devoid of hope* where it seemed like none of my efforts would ever pay off, that I was destined to keep re-experiencing this pain. I vividly remember discussing this in a therapy session, expressing intense frustration that I had fallen into this hole yet again, when suddenly I "saw" an image of a wooden ladder positioned so that it stuck out several feet above the hole. I'd never seen this ladder before. With this image in my mind, I recognized that there was a way for me to climb out of the hole, and that I could do so anytime I slipped back in there, which made my fears, and frustration much easier to deal with. This knowledge dramatically changed the experience of healing for me, as it represented hope, and literally a way to climb out of my pain. I encourage you to be open to healing in *whatever form it takes*, and with the expectation that you may be pleasantly surprised with the results.

While the focus up to this point has been on surviving and healing from the experience of being raised by a ghost mother, it's within your reach to *thrive* from what you've been through, as a direct result of all that you'll learn on this journey. I first became aware of this possibility when I came across a book titled, **Legacy of the Heart: The Spiritual Advantages of a Painful Childhood**, by Wayne Muller. *What is this man talking about? I wondered; how could this be so?* This surely hadn't been my experience. *He must be nuts*, I concluded, but in spite of my skepticism I bought the book. I was immediately hooked when I read the following: *I . . .*

noted that adults who were hurt as children inevitably exhibit a peculiar strength, a profound inner wisdom, and a remarkable creativity and insight. Deep within them-just beneath the wound-lies a profound spiritual vitality, a quiet knowing, a way of perceiving what is beautiful, right and true. This is an insightful, uplifting book; I encourage you to read it when you're ready.

Now I want to share some similar thoughts in this regard—think of this as *advanced healing strategies* to help you understand, and appreciate life in amazing ways. Even if these ideas seem impossible based on how you are currently feeling, there is considerable hope in considering this perspective, in knowing that there are real gifts hidden in the pain of this experience.

Learning to Appreciate the Gifts of a Ghost Mother

Thinking about these concepts has reminded me of when, as a teenager, I participated in The Outward Bound School. During this time spent in the mountains of North Carolina, I received an important lesson about how to use my thoughts to my advantage. This occurred when, after hiking uphill for hours, I began saying to myself, *I can't go any farther, if I do I'm gonna puke, or keel over.* These thoughts made me feel like giving up, because in reality neither of these things was happening. One of the leaders sensed my distress and offered the advice to focus on the progress I was making, rather than on the goal of finishing the day's hike; and she added it would help to hold onto the belief that I could keep going until we reached our destination. What a difference following her advice made in my ability to keep putting one foot in front of the other, no matter how weary I felt, or how long our group needed to hike to get to the next campsite.

Healing is a very personal experience, one that requires curiosity and belief in the power of change. In coming to terms with all that you've learned, including the strength and inner resolve it's taken to get to this point, you now have the opportunity to launch yourself into a different way of being alive. So much of what we have to do to heal from a ghost mother feels *counterintuitive;* for example, having to let go of her when part of us still wants to hold on tight. Yet, the keys to this healing journey are found in listening to our intuition, our inner sense of knowing. In doing so, our healing takes on a life of its own, and comes in unexpected ways, such as meeting gifted healers, finding a book or poem that speaks to us, or connecting with someone who has suffered in the same ways.

Once you begin to reach a point of peace in dealing with your ghost mother, and see the benefits of strengthening your own spirit, you're likely to be introduced to possibilities that previously didn't even occur to you. What you learned when you had to dig deep, in order to cope and essentially raise yourself, continues to contribute to your development. Whatever your specific circumstances, I know that you've had to tap into a considerable amount of courage, and strength, in order to have gotten this far. Having the ability to survive a ghost mother has taught you unique skills in managing emotional pain, and continuing to move forward against all odds.

There is additional instruction in this regard, if you are open to it, to include connecting with others through the experience of healing, accepting that life unfolds in mysterious ways, deep appreciation for the caring of others, and gratitude for finding your way through this pain. By focusing on understanding and living life on a deeper level, as a result of growing up with a ghost mother, remarkable gifts are revealed, and we get to take a journey that otherwise might not have been taken.

To exemplify these gifts, here are some that appear on my list titled, *What I've Learned in Healing From my Ghost Mother:*

- **We each have life lessons to learn, and also to teach.**

- **I'm more powerful than I ever thought possible, I get to decide how to live my life and what's important to me.**

- **The amazing courage inside me, evidenced in my ability to stick with this process, and to speak my truth.**

- The rewards and beauty of the mother-daughter relationship, by creating a strong connection with my daughter.

- The compassion to accept that as humans we are flawed, imperfect.

- To refrain from trying to change other people, and not to expect them to provide what they aren't capable of giving.

- That carrying around resentment and anger is harmful to me.

- The ability to love myself, and to feel deserving of love from others.

- Deep empathy for others who are suffering.

- The inner strength to see a difficult situation as it truly is, and the knowledge that I have the ability to deal with it.

Now don't misunderstand what I'm saying, I did not learn these lessons directly *from* my ghost mother, I learned them in the process of accepting, and working through the pain created as the result of being raised by her; by making the choice to take responsibility for developing into the person I wanted to become. Do I wish that I been raised by a real mother? You bet I do. I know the extent of the pain, confusion and torment I've dealt with in being raised by a ghost, and having to figure out ways to get what I didn't receive growing up. I'm not advocating that anyone go out in search of a ghost mother, but I also can't ignore the powerful lessons that I've learned in my efforts to move forward, or how fantastic it feels to successfully navigate this journey. I want you to know the wonderful lessons this healing can reveal; how much it has to teach about appreciation for being alive, and the ability to love, and be loved.

When I asked the women who've contributed their stories to consider the positive lessons learned from their ghost mother, all agreed this was a challenge, but it's one they eagerly accepted. I really appreciate the insights they came up with, and think you will too:

POSITIVE LESSONS LEARNED FROM A GHOST MOTHER

- **How to rely on myself.**

- **To take responsibility for myself, and my actions.**

- **To trust my instincts and intuition for guidance.**

- **I've become more aware of human vulnerabilities, including my own.**

- **That no one has a perfect childhood.**

- I rejoice that I will never again put up with being mistreated.

- Spiritually, it has helped me to find my own path.

- The value of giving to others from the heart.

- To teach myself what I need to learn.

- How to survive disappointments.

- To cherish things about myself that make me happy.

- I think I'm more open-minded to diversity in people.

- It's heightened my awareness of receiving affection that is genuine.

- I've learned how to create good compatibility with others.

- How to respect personal boundaries.

- Motivation to live a better life.

- A strong desire to raise my kids better.

- **An intuitive sense of what I need to do to survive.**

- **I'm filled with hope for a better life.**

- **I've learned resilience.**

- **That self-pity is not an attractive quality, so I don't go there.**

- **Not to buy into limiting beliefs.**

- **That my journey is ongoing.**

- **Good friends who care and understand me are a salvation.**

- **I have choices about how I respond.**

I imagine that all ghost daughters wish we'd been raised by a mother who loved, nurtured and supported us, but because of all we've been through, there is now a passionate appreciation for the people and events in life that *are* real. These gifts are within your reach, all available to you. You deserve them and it's your birthright to receive them, this is the light at the end of the tunnel when you make a commitment to stick with the process of healing from a ghost mother.

Moving Beyond the Shadow of a Ghost Mother

It's interesting to consider that our mothers are, in many ways, victimized by their own illusiveness, and would probably prefer to be happier, and better connected to their children. From a deeply spiritual perspective that believes in reincarnation, there is the viewpoint that these mothering issues are necessary for her to learn the required lessons for this lifetime. To take this a step further, perhaps these are the lessons we need to learn in this lifetime as well. The first time I heard the expression, *you choose your parents*, I was horrified, but it is an interesting concept to ponder. *What if* the pain for all involved in this experience is part of a divine design to teach and inspire us?

I'm a mental health therapist, not a spiritual guru, but what I know for sure is that exploring these issues from a more enlightened perspective has helped me to understand, and come to terms with my pain, and I encourage you to consider exploring all that spiritual teachings have to offer. These aren't the "woo-woo" concepts that some people assume them to be; in simple terms spirituality is the pursuit of personal development through the exploration of universal values and meaning. This is an approach that encourages meditation, prayer, contemplation, and self-reflection. It can be accessed through books, CD's, the practice of yoga, meditation, participation in a spiritual community, and many other ways. This exploration has comforted me and broadened my thinking, in addition to connecting me with others determined to heal, and providing the tools to transcend problems that previously seemed insurmountable.

What I've learned is that the more you learn to trust, appreciate and listen to the intuition that has helped you survive the turmoil you've experienced, the more you're able to access deeper levels of healing, and living. These are the hidden gifts of having to deal with this pain. Ultimately, your ability to accept your ghost mother's limitations, and to move past her illusiveness, leads to the creation of a rich environment for healing that stands in stark contrast to how you grew up. In this new way of living, you truly appreciate being treated kindly by others, acknowledge yourself as a powerful person, and see wonderful possibilities for the future.

To get outstanding results requires making a commitment to yourself; that moving beyond the pain of the past is a priority, essential to your continued growth and happiness. It's important to appreciate each piece of progress you make, and to embrace lessons learned from both your brain, and your heart. Be kind to yourself as you heal, set a goal of *progress not perfection*, as the AA saying goes. The process of healing takes time; there will be times when you can't keep up with the changes you're making, and other times when it feels like you're getting nowhere. This is how healing works, and keep in mind how tightly bound the knot is that you are working to untangle. It took many years to develop this ghost pain, now take the time needed to let go of your past, and replace it with a new and improved reality. Developing your strong spirit requires patience, persistence and a sense of humor.

Your situation, and sense of self, will continue to improve as long as you stay focused on moving forward. It's reassuring, and exciting, to know that not only can your current circumstances improve, but you can also look forward to feeling happy, content, and empowered. It would have helped me so much to know that the battle I fought for so long would have a happy ending; that continuing to force myself to face my pain would have a payoff that was worth *all* the effort.

This is the primary message I want to convey as we come to the end of this book; stick with the process of healing and don't settle for an illusive, painful existence. Embrace your healing; see it as an opportunity for growth and learning. The gifts you discover in your journey are likely to surprise you, and very likely to exceed the suffering you've gone through in your journey to reach them. You are not alone. Learn from your past, and then leave it behind.

I extend my hope for your profound healing, and that you no longer feel haunted. Surviving a ghost mother is good; thriving is even better. Your pain will propel you to search for answers; the answers will create a strength deep inside you that will forever change your life.

~*Love After Love, by Derek Walcott*~

The time will come when,
with elation
you will greet yourself arriving
at your own door, in your own mirror,
and each will smile at the other's welcome.
And say sit here. Eat.
You will love again the stranger
Who was yourself.
Give wine, to the stranger who has loved you.
All your life, whom you ignored
for another, who knows you by heart.
Take down the love letters from the bookshelf.
The photographs, the desperate notes.
Peel your own image from the mirror.
Sit. Feast on your life.

EPILOGUE

It is my sincere hope that this book contributes to your ability to make powerful changes in coming to terms with the difficulties in being raised by a ghost mother. I also hope that the sharing of my experience, and the strategies I've developed, will help in educating mental health professionals to better meet the needs of women who have been ghost mothered. This has been an incredible opportunity to create a blueprint for healing from this insidious pain, and I'm grateful for the chance to do so.

I have found it challenging to decide how much personal information to divulge, but I consider myself so fortunate in having healed from this pain that it seems I had no choice but to put in writing all that I've learned. Even with this clarity, I had to ask myself whether it is fair to disclose so much about my mother, and what I've been through with her. Obviously, all that I've written is from my own perspective. I recognize that she doesn't see this situation in the same way, but after all, isn't that the point? Ghost mothers, by definition, live in the world in a way that supports their own reality, but not that of others—especially not their children. I have wrestled with my role and responsibility in portraying ghost mothers, have thought carefully about the assumptions I made, and always chose my focus based on the goal of decreasing the suffering of others struggling with this pain.

Writing this book has been therapeutic for me in ways I did not anticipate, and suggests that my healing journey will never be over; it will just continue to get more interesting. Reflecting on all that I've learned, I've come to realize that I'm no longer angry with my ghost mother, and have finally stopped longing for her. I have cried, screamed, and worked through my grief for the mother I never had. These days I barely recognize my own life; it's truly amazing how much my inner, and outer, realities have changed since making the decision 15 years ago to heal from the pain in my maternal relationship.

At that dark time in my life I felt so powerless, and would NEVER have believed there was light at the end of the tunnel, much less an entirely different way of viewing the world, and my place in it. I continue to be in awe of this reality, that underneath pain and suffering, there is healing and self-awareness. Being so fortunate in this regard I really didn't expect the Universe to continue to support my efforts when I discovered my passion for sharing this information with other ghost daughters. It seems I don't give the Universe enough credit because everything has easily fallen into place. I learned so much, and was so inspired by Dr. Karyl McBride. I was quickly offered the opportunity to rent office space from my chiropractors, and met my literary agent quite by accident. All "divine appointments," Dr. Carolle would say.

The opportunity to use what I've learned to encourage other women brings me a sense of joy I never thought I would find. My daughter has grown up and is pursuing her dreams of flying—literally—which gives me even more time to focus on helping to heal others, while I continue the daily practice of healing myself. My husband strongly supports my efforts to turn years of angst into something positive, and has a pragmatic viewpoint that helps balance my right-brained approach.

While I don't recommend growing up with a ghost mother, doing so has surely shaped me into the person that I am today. I am hopeful that there will be increased opportunities for others to grow from the pain of a ghost mother, as the impact of this lack of nurturing continues to be brought out of the shadows. I intend to stay deeply involved in this process, sharing my experience and strategies, educating mental health professionals, and continuing to come up with new ghost information and ideas. My wish for you is for your profound healing, and happiness.

RECOMMENDED RESOURCES

(Website links are listed on www.ghostmothers.com)

Books About Problematic Maternal Relationships

- The Emotionally Absent Mother: *A Guide to Self-Healing and Getting the Love You Missed*, by Jasmin Lee Cori, M.S., L.P.C

- Toxic Parents: *Overcoming Their Hurtful Legacy and Reclaiming Your Life*, by Susan Forward, Ph.D.

- Mean Mothers: *Overcoming the Legacy of Hurt*, by Peg Streep

- Bad Childhood, Good Life, by Dr. Laura Schlessinger

- Difficult Mothers, by Terri Apter

Books About Narcissistic Mothers

- Will I Ever Be Good Enough? *Healing the Daughters of Narcissistic Mothers*, by Karyl McBride, Ph.D.

- Children of the Self-Absorbed: *A Grownup's Guide to Getting Over Narcissistic Parents*, by Nina W. Brown, Ed.D., L.P.C

- Trapped in the Mirror: *Adult Children of Narcissists in Their Struggle For Self*, by Elan Golomb, Ph.D.

Books and CD's About Healing

- Healing the Shame That Binds You, by John Bradshaw

- Whose Life is it Anyway? *When to Stop Taking Care of Their Feelings and Start Taking Care of Your Own*, by Nina W. Brown, Ed.D, LPC, NCC

- You Can Heal Your Life, by Louise Hay

- The Hoffman Process: *The World Famous Technique That Empowers You to Forgive Your Past, Heal Your Present, and Transform Your Future*, by Tim Laurence

Healing Resources With a Spiritual Perspective

- Legacy of the Heart: *The Spiritual Advantages of a Painful Childhood*, by Wayne Muller

- Mind, Body, Soul and Money: *Putting Your Life in Balance*, by Carolle Jean-Murat, M.D.

- Ask Yourself This: *Questions to Open the Heart, Expand the Mind and Awaken the Soul*, by Rev. Wendy Craig-Purcell

Resources for Dealing With Anger

- Anger Releasing (CD), by Louise Hay

- The Dance of Anger: *A Woman's Guide To Changing The Patterns of Intimate Relationships*, by Harriet Lerner, Ph.D.

Improving Self-Esteem

- Self-Esteem: *Your Fundamental Power* (CD), by Carolyn Myss

- Self-Esteem: *A Proven Program of Cognitive Techniques for Assessing, Improving and Maintaining Your*

> *Self-Esteem*, by Matthew McKay PhD, and Patrick
> Fanning

- Self-Esteem Affirmations: *Motivational Affirmations
  for Building Confidence and Recognizing Self-Worth*
  (CD), by Louise Hay

Healing Techniques (Links are listed on my website)

- B.E.S.T (Bio Energetic Synchronization Technique)

- Cognitive-Behavioral Therapy—National Association
  of Cognitive-Behavioral Therapists

- EFT (Emotional Freedom Techniques)

- EMDR (Eye Movement Desensitization and
  Reprocessing)

- Hypnosis—American Society of Clinical Hypnosis

- Yoga Therapy (Phoenix Rising)

Locate Mental Health Professionals in Your Area

- Therapists specializing in issues related to being poorly
  mothered, listed on Dr. McBride's website.

- The Therapist Directory: presented by Psychology Today.

- Association for Behavioral and Cognitive Therapies.

Support Groups

- CoDA—Co-Dependents Anonymous (12-step model)

- ACA—Adult Children of Alcoholics (12-step model)

Additional Resources

- Dr. Karyl McBride's website for Daughters of Narcissistic Mothers

- The Power of Forgiveness: *How to Set Yourself Free From Past Traumas* (E-book by Dr. Carolle Jean-Murat)

- Are You As Happy As Your Dog? *Sure-Fire Ways to Wake Up With a Smile as Big as Your Pooch's*, by Alan Cohen.

- Guided Mindfulness Meditation Series 1, by Jon Kabat-Zinn (CD)

- Letting Go Of Stress: *Four Effective Techniques for Relaxation and Stress Reduction*, by Emmett Miller, M.D., and Steven Halpern (CD)

- Songs for the Inner Child, by Shaina Noll (CD)

- American Tai Chi and Qigong Association

ABOUT THE AUTHOR

Kathryn Rudlin, LCSW has credentials as both a mental health professional, and a professional writer. Since 1988, she has worked in California as a Licensed Clinical Social Worker (LCSW), having completed her Masters Degree in Social Work (MSW) at The University of Denver, a Bachelors Degree (BA) in Psychology at The American University, Washington DC, post-graduate courses in family therapy, and clinical supervision, and was personally trained by Dr. Karyl McBride in her recovery model for daughters of narcissistic mothers. She has worked at every level of therapeutic treatment to include foster care, alternative schools, residential treatment, wilderness therapy, and psychiatric hospitals.

Kathryn is a member of the National Association of Social Workers (NASW), the Endometriosis Association, and the Unity Center of San Diego. As a professional writer she has published articles in the NASW California newsletter, San Diego Woman Magazine, and is a widely read contributing writer for About.com/A New York Times Company, on the topic of troubled teens. In addition, she has written a workbook on effective group therapy with adolescents, created bi-lingual learning materials for children, and was co-owner of Clinical Inspiration, a company that developed continuing education materials for mental health professionals. Recently she edited Dr. Carolle Jean-Murat's book, Voodoo in My Blood: A Healer's Journey From Surgeon to Shaman.

The book *Ghost Mothers* was inspired by the many years Kathryn spent trying to create a positive relationship with her illusive mother. When years of effort led nowhere, she came to see that her mother wasn't capable of maternal nurturing, and that she was now a ghost daughter, haunted by painful feelings, and memories from being raised this way. This shift in understanding helped her to heal, and to recognize her passion for helping others do the same.

Currently, she is a therapist in private practice in San Diego, specializing in counseling and education for daughters with ghost mother issues, in addition to providing training on this topic to mental health professionals.

Specialized training in treating ghost daughters:

- Healing the Daughter's of Narcissistic Mothers, 3-day workshop presented by Dr. Karyl McBride

- Healing From Loss and Abandonment, presented by Claudia Black, Ph.D.

- Emotional Manipulation: Understanding Manipulators and Helping Their Victims, Presented by James A. Fogarty, Ed.D.

- Narcissistic Personality Disorder, presented by Patricia Patton, Ph.D.

- Personality Disorders in Social Work and Health Care, presented by Gregory W. Lester, Ph.D.

- Borderline Personality Disorders, presented by speakers to include Sandy Hotchkiss, LCSW, and Christine Lawson, Ph.D.

Contact Information:

I welcome your comments, and questions, related to healing from a ghost mother, contact me directly at:

krudlinlcsw@att.net

For more information visit my website:
www.ghostmothers.com

Kathryn Rudlin, LCSW
10175 Rancho Carmel Drive
Suite 116
San Diego, CA 92128

ABOUT
DR. CAROLLE JEAN-MURAT,

Fluent in five languages, born and raised in Haiti in a family with shamanic roots, educated in Haiti, Mexico, Jamaica, and the U.S., Dr. Carolle Jean-Murat is a medical intuitive, a board-certified gynecologist, a senior fellow of the American College of Obstetricians and Gynecologists, a menopause specialist, seminar leader, and award-winning author. She has over three decades of experience in women's health. Dr. Carolle had a successful holistic private practice as a board-certified Ob-Gyn in San Diego from 1982 until 2005.

Her success as a doctor working in the traditional medical model became increasingly problematic as she could intuitively see the source of her patient's problems as often being due to emotional, rather than physical causes. Since 2005 she has been offering "Life Decisions with Clarity", intuitive consultations provided at Dr. Carolle's Wellness and Retreat Center of San Diego, that are designed to advise women at a crossroads in their life. She also provides intuitive medical consultations, expert second opinions, and one-on-one private, and group retreats to help women better understand their symptoms, health needs, and best options for holistic treatment, and lifestyle adjustments. During a session by phone, or in person, Dr. Carolle is able to provide guidance and support in bringing emotions to consciousness, and dealing with them effectively.

Dr. Carolle has worked extensively with female veterans who suffer from post-traumatic stress disorder (PTSD) due to sexual trauma during their military experience, to include in-depth assessments, providing specialized alternative treatments, and testifying on their behalf. For over two decades, Dr. Carolle has provided free medical care to underserved women through Catholic Charities, St. Vincent de Paul Village, and

Native-American Health programs. In 1993 she founded the 501(c)-3 non-profit organization, Health Through Communications Foundation to provide education, health-care, and hope for the future.

Accompanied by a team of doctors, and other medical personal, Dr. Carolle frequently travels to La Vallée de Jacmel, Haiti to provide free medical care, medical supplies, and develop preventive health programs. In spite of the setbacks suffered during the devastating 2010 earthquake, she works tirelessly to raise funds that will create the needed infrastructure to provide a foundation for creating self-sufficient, productive, and thriving communities. As an international motivational speaker, Dr. Carolle brings her message of self-empowerment to women through her award-winning books, her blog, lectures, webinars, seminars, magazines, newspapers, and appearances on radio and TV.

Books by Dr. Carolle:

- Moving Beyond Sexual Trauma: A Victim No More! Coming soon.
- Voodoo in My Blood: A Healer's Journey From Surgeon to Shaman—Coming this fall.
- Is It My Hormones—Or Is It Something Else: How to find out what's REALLY causing your physical, mental, and emotional symptoms—and what to do about it. Coming soon.
- *Award-winning* Menopause Made Easy: How to Make the Right Decisions for the Rest of Your Life—with a chapter on Healthy Aging by Louise L. Hay, published by Hay House 1999. French version 2008 La Ménopause Démystifiée: Comment prendre des décisions éclairées pour le reste de votre vie.
- Mind, Body, Soul & Money: Putting Your Life in Balance, Mosley Publishing, 2002.
- Natural Pregnancy A-Z, published by Hay House, 2000.

How to contact Dr. Carolle:

www.drcarolle.com

drcarolle@cox.net

619-850-5030